TACKLE ANGLING

GW00707799

Tackle Angling

JOHN MICHAELSON

Revised by Brian Harris,
Editor of *Angling* Magazine

STANLEY PAUL
London

STANLEY PAUL & CO LTD
3 Fitzroy Square, London W1

An imprint of the Hutchinson Publishing Group

London Melbourne Sydney Auckland
Wellington Johannesburg Cape Town
and agencies throughout the world

First published 1959
Second impression 1961
Third impression 1962
Fourth impression 1968
Fifth impression 1971
Revised edition 1974
© John Michaelson 1959

Set in Monotype Times, printed in Great Britain by
The Anchor Press Ltd, and bound by
Wm. Brendon & Son Ltd, both of Tiptree, Essex

ISBN 0 09 120450 x (cased)
0 09 120451 8 (paper)

Contents

Illustrations

ACKNOWLEDGEMENTS

*The Author acknowledges his thanks for permission to
reproduce the following illustrations: Nos. 3, 4, 8 and 9, by
courtesy of Radio Times Hulton Picture Library; No. 1,
Ronald Goodearl; Nos. 5 and 6, boro failce eireann, Dublin;
Nos. 10 and 15, Scottish Tourist Board; No. 11, The Times;
Nos. 12 and 13. Norway Travel Association; No. 14,
O.F.V.W. Baumgartner; No. 2, S. Keal; No. 7, A. Nevison.*

DIAGRAMS

Introduction

If the popularity of a sport is judged by the number of those who practise it as distinct from the number who watch, angling is now the most popular sport in Britain and probably in the world. And it is becoming more popular every year. Basically this may be because angling satisfies in a civilized way the primitive instinct of the chase. But the actual motives which make so many men and an increasing number of women take up angling are as varied as the ways in which they practise the sport. The variety of activities we describe with the word 'angling' explains its appeal to all kinds and conditions of people.

For some, angling means sitting with intense concentration at a pegged spot on a featureless canal for four or five hours during which not a second must be wasted in anything but catching fish in competition with hundreds of other anglers. For others it means wading in solitude up a boulder-strewn stream, the pleasure coming as much from the fresh air, exercise, scenery and sound of the water as from the weight of the creel. Angling may mean sitting in a boat drifting silently down a lake or standing on a rock against which the waves are beating noisily.

Angling is an individual sport, but it can be solitary or sociable as the angler chooses. It can be the cheapest of all sports or one of the most expensive. And who shall say that the angler taking home two or three fish from a beach which have cost him nothing has any less pleasure than the man whose week's salmon-fishing costs him a hundred pounds?

In keeping with the trend in every sport, angling has an increasing number of specialists. There is the match fisherman whose high degree of specialized skill may extend to attracting fish away from his neighbour and the tournament caster who makes angling almost an athletic field event, his sport as different from the average angler's as a racing motorist's circling of the track is from an afternoon run in the family car. There are anglers who specialize in techniques and in individual species of fish, and men who say that if they cannot catch fish by one particular method they would rather not catch them at all. Some used to live only for the June to September period, when they went carp fishing. Now, of course, winter fishing for carp has been proved to be reasonably successful.

Bringing one skill to perfection and specialization can give great satisfaction. And as family-motoring benefits from motor-racing, so the great body of ordinary anglers owe a great deal to the specialists. But angling is a sport and a relaxation, and its fullest pleasures, I feel, are enjoyed by the all-rounder. The angler who seeks all fish and knows many techniques need never deny himself a day's sport because it is the wrong time of the year or he cannot reach a particular spot. This is particularly the case in Britain with its extraordinary and probably unique variety of fishing waters. Almost anywhere in the country an angler has within an hour or two's journey waters varying from crystal chalk streams to canals, and from natural lakes to carefully stocked reservoirs. When we consider the variety of fishing to be found in almost any hundred square miles of the country, it is not surprising British anglers have mastered a greater number of techniques than those of other countries.

Not the least of the rewards of the all-round angler is the varied scenery he comes to know. The reed-beds and peaceful water-meadows of a southern chalk stream; the placid midland canal seeking its way through rolling hills; the river fed by a hundred rivulets tumbling down from the mountains; the reservoir formed by flooding a valley which now looks as if it had been there since the beginning of time; the broads and fens that seem to stretch to the horizon; even the great river flowing through an industrial area which is transformed by the magic of a midsummer dawn. The angler who seeks new waters will in the course of a few seasons find himself enjoying a greater variety of natural beauty than would be possible in any other country in the world.

Some angling literature almost suggests that actually catching fish is a mere incidental to botany, bird-watching or communing with Nature. But, to get full satisfaction from his sport, the average angler wants something in his creel or keep-net at the end of the day and it is from this viewpoint that this book is written. The all-round angler will not often achieve the records of the specialists. But there is no reason why he should not acquire sufficient mastery of every technique and knowledge of every fish and type of water to ensure pleasure from his sport at all times of the year and in any place. The purpose of this book is to provide sufficient basic knowledge of the angler's fishes and their environment and the techniques of catching them to enable the intelligent angler to be successful anywhere.

I

Getting to Know Fish

THE whole of angling can be summed up in a sentence. It consists in deceiving a fish into seizing what it takes to be a meal in such a way that it can be taken out of the water by the angler. This may seem obvious, but the essential point of deception often seems to be overlooked in all the elaborate paraphernalia of tackle and techniques. Successful deception requires knowledge of how fish live, act and think. Part of the fascination of angling is that it requires entry into a complete different environment, the world of water instead of the world of air we take for granted. At the point where your line penetrates the surface of the water, you are exploring a world completely different from your own.

In recent years skin-diving has made it possible for men to get personal knowledge of this world of water and much knowledge valuable to anglers has resulted. But the angler can enter the fish's world only by imagination based on knowledge. We describe the senses of fish by the same words as we use for our own—sight, touch, hearing, taste and smell. But the organs of sense in fish and the way in which they are used are in many ways quite different. The angler must understand the senses of fish, for it is through them the fish becomes aware of his lure and is warned of his tackle and presence.

There is a difference in the 'attitude' of the fish and of the angler. The angler is aware of the fish as a fish and that it is his quarry. The fish is not aware of the angler or his purpose. Even the most 'educated' fish in a hard-fished water is incapable of thinking: 'That is a Man and I know I must be

13

careful because he is trying to catch me.' Some writers describe the thoughts of fishes in human terms like this, but it is safe to say that a fish does not think in the way we commonly use the word. When the shadow of an aeroplane falls across a stream, a trout darts to safety as 'unthinkingly' as if the shadow had been that of an angler's rod, in response to a reflex we may guess has been built up through countless generations of fish which have lived literally under the shadows of herons or other predatory birds.

Trying to put yourself into the mind of the fish will make for better angling and incidentally add greatly to the interest of your sport. The dry-fly fisherman, with his close visual contact with his quarry, is continually trying to consider his lure from the fish's point of view, but this is no less important, even if more difficult, for the angler who rarely sees a fish until it is brought to the net.

What may be the most important sense organ of fish is one of which we have no equivalent. The lateral line is so-called because it runs from the middle of the tail to the gill covers on both sides of the fish's body. If you look carefully you may see the rows of pierced scales. The organ continues into the head more deeply. In the pike, where it seems particularly well developed, you will notice pores on the head which are the external connections.

The use of this organ has been the subject of a lot of speculation and little proof. But it may not be far wrong to think of it as a sort of sonar, like the electronic device used for detecting submarines and carrying out soundings. It is sensitive to low-frequency vibrations well below the minimum of sixteen per second which the human ear interprets as sound. The lateral line may enable a fish to 'feel' objects with which it is not in actual contact—the push of a current or its deflection from stone or bank or even another fish. It may be what enables a fish to keep station, apparently without effort, responding automatically to the smallest

14

changes in water pressure. It could explain why a blind fish does not run ashore or collide with the bank.

From the angler's viewpoint of deception, its importance is probably that it enables a fish to be aware of movements outside its range of vision or hearing in the ordinary sense. It is probably not the splash of a wading angler or the sound of a boot on the bank that reaches a fish, but the low-frequency vibrations set up in the water or earth. The sound of a rod being laid on a stand may seem trifling to the angler but reach a fish some distance away in terms of movement on the bank. The louder cough or conversation of the angler may not reach it at all. I have seen a trout undisturbed by the discharge of a shot-gun into the air, but put down by the butt being grounded.

It is not certain whether fish hear sounds in the normal range of the human ear. They have an organ corresponding to the inner ear, but there is no external connection and it may be much more concerned with balance than receiving high-frequency vibrations in the water. When the angler is advised not to frighten fish by making a noise, he must remember that the noise which disturbs a fish is the low-frequency vibration. It is more important to tread softly than to speak softly.

Fish have taste buds in their mouths, and if it has barbels there will also be taste buds on them, suggesting these little projections round the mouth help in finding food as much by taste as by touch. The importance of taste is obvious, but the allied sense of smell is often overlooked. Water passing through what we call the nostrils of the fish touches nerve endings and the sense of smell plays an important and perhaps often decisive part in the fish's decision whether something is good to eat, not merely in the positive sense that it is food, but also that it is safe. A bait that has been put on the hook by tobacco-contaminated fingers may be refused not because the fish dislikes tobacco but because the smell is unusual and therefore arouses supicion and fear.

You should take care that your baits, especially those that have no pronounced smell of their own, are free from contamination. There is reason to think fish can detect a smell at some distance and that it could be used to attract them. The sea-angler knows the value of pilchard and herring oil for making a variety of baits attractive and if a whole dead fish is used, it is worth scoring it lightly to release the taste and smell. The possibilities of using smell as well as taste, texture and appearance to make freshwater baits attractive are a fascinating subject for experiment (see chapter on Coarse Fish and Baits).

My attention was drawn to the subject when as a boy I was fishing one of the upper reaches of the Tamar without much success. I met a farmer and looking enviously at his basket of trout said I supposed I had better change my fly. 'Don't change 'un, christen 'un,' he said, and while I watched, puzzled, he rubbed my wet fly in the open mouth of one of his fish. Squeezing it more or less clean, he gave it back to me. The superstition of a countryman, I thought, but the next hour yielded half a dozen fish where before I had none.

It could have been coincidence, of course, but thinking it over I wondered whether 'christening' the fly had not given it a positive smell rather than an absence of smell and thus just tipped the scales in favour of its acceptance by a suspicious fish. Many anglers have noticed that when they have taken one fish, others seem to follow more easily, and attributed this to the fish 'coming on to feed'. But the fact that the fly has already touched one fish may be significant. So many factors may be involved in the acceptance or rejection of a bait that it is hard to prove the value of anything designed to appeal to the fish's sense of smell. But such things as using a little of the contents of the stomach of the first fish caught to mix paste, or even touching baits with the slime from the mouth of a fish, are worth trying.

In most cases it is probably through the sense of sight that

1. Fishing from the apron of a weir is often particularly good early in the season when roach and chub may be taken as well as barbel. This weir is on the Thames at Hambleden

2. A light, modern, hollow glass rod suitable for roach,
in battle with a barbel

the attention of a fish is first drawn to a lure or bait—or of the angler. An understanding of how and what a fish sees is essential to successful angling. It is difficult for us to get the fish's point of view because there are important differences between its eyes and our own and because it sees in a different medium. The science of vision has now been studied in great detail in laboratories and we probably know all that dissection and optics can tell us. But science can reveal only *how* a fish sees, not *what* it sees. That we can guess only by imaginative inference from experience.

The proportion of the brain of a fish which is concerned with sight is relatively large. We can infer that its vision is acute and good in what we should regard as a bad light. At dawn and dusk or in deep water, fish probably see better than we do. It is difficult to approach a fish in sunshine, unless it is in deep water, not so much because the strong light enables it to see better as because the slightest movements of rod, nylon or any other hard surface are liable to produce what to the fish seem strong flashes of light, although the angler himself may not notice them. The angler should beware of casting a shadow on the water where the fish is positioned. But if shadows are avoided, it is now fairly certain that it is easier to approach fish in sunlight than in dull conditions, probably because they are dazzled— for the reasons given below.

Fish have no eyelids. They cannot close or narrow their eyes against a strong light. They can protect themselves against light they find unpleasantly strong only by moving out of it into shade or into deeper water where most of the light will be scattered or absorbed by suspended particles before it reaches them. On sunny days we shall find fish in the shade of trees or the bank or in deeper parts of the water.

Human vision is binocular, the two eyes working together. By moving them and by turning our head, we get a very wide field of vision, almost a complete circle without having to move our body. Each eye of a fish works separately and can only be rotated to a very limited degree. To alter its field of view substantially, a fish must move its whole body, not merely its head. This field of vision is an arc of about 150 degrees on each side and there are blind spots behind, above and in front, the exact size of which depends on the shape of the particular species. The blind area behind is roughly one which makes an angle of about fifty degrees at the fish's nose. This makes it possible to approach a fish from behind unseen (but not unheard!). Since fish normally lie with their heads facing the direction of the current, this means they are most easily approached upstream. Beware fish in eddies facing downstream!

Unlike the human eye, that of the fish has little accommodation. It cannot be altered in shape like ours to bring objects at greatly varying distances into proper focus. Taken with monocular vision, this probably means fish cannot see objects stereoscopically or in depth and that it can examine them in detail only at a comparatively short and fixed distance. But against this, a fish can look at two objects on different sides at the same time and it does not require to see details to note sudden changes in the light due to the movement of reflecting surfaces at considerable distances. These flashes telling of the movement of some object are, so to speak, the fish's distant warning signals.

Scientists have said that fish cannot see colours in the way we do. But if fish are colour-blind in the human sense, experiments with coloured feeding vessels, not to mention the experience of anglers, show they can distinguish between objects similar in every respect except colour. A fish may not take a maggot because it is red, but a maggot dyed red may in certain conditions be more visible or attractive than one in its natural colour. Another point to bear in mind, especially when selecting artificial lures, is that the colour of an object submerged in water may be quite different from its colour in air.

There is another fundamental difference between the visual world of fish and our own, of special importance to the fly-fisherman, but not to be neglected by any angler. We look at things almost wholly in one medium, the air. Fish are concerned with objects in two mediums, the water in which they live and the world of air beyond from which it is divided by the surface of the water. When light passes from one medium to the other, it is refracted or bent, so that the line connecting the eye of the fish and the eye of the angler is not straight and neither sees the other in their real position. Everyone is familiar with the apparent bending of a stick, when it is half-pushed into water. Of course, it is not the stick which is bent but the rays of light reflected from it passing through the surface of the water. To a fish, an object outside its world of water always appears higher and nearer than it really is. To the angler, a fish always looks further away and nearer the surface than it really is.

But light rays striking the water at a narrow angle (less than ten degrees) do not penetrate at all. They glance off and, as far as the fish is concerned, make no impression because they do not reach its eyes. Without going into the rather complicated optics of the matter, this means that a fish's vision into the world of air is limited to a 'window'. When we approach a window, we increase our field of vision outside it. But a fish's field of vision increases as it retreats from the surface window. Fortunately for the angler water scatters and absorbs light, and the narrower the angle at which light strikes the surface the less penetrates. A fish at a considerable depth with a large window may therefore see little or nothing of objects on the bank because insufficient light from them reaches its eyes.

An obvious deduction is that it is easier to approach a fish unseen if you keep low. By halving your height by bending or crawling, you can reduce the distance at which you become theoretically visible to a fish near the surface from about twenty-three to fifteen yards. But you must not forget your rod. If you wave a shiny rod six feet above your head you may alarm a fish as effectively as if you had walked boldly upright.

I say wave the rod, because it is the movement of an object rather than its mere presence which alarms fish. There is no more reason why a fish should take fright at a man standing motionless than it should at a tree. If you have the patience to remain motionless on the bank of a clear stream long enough, you can watch fish feeding unconcerned within a few feet of you, a fascinating and instructive exercise for the angler. The moment you move, the fish will be gone.

How easily movement is noticed depends on the background. If your background is much the same tone as that of your clothes, your movements are less likely to be noticed, even though you may be well within the field of view of the fish. Movements are generally most obvious when they are made against the light background of the sky and you are more likely to alarm fish if you wear white or brightly coloured clothes which reflect light. Not because fish dislike white or red objects, but because any movement of them will catch the fish's attention. I have never met an angler with his face darkened like a commando, but it would be quite logical, and I have sometimes wondered how many fish have been alarmed by light flashing from my glasses.

The rules for being unnoticed are simple in principle. Keep low, try to blend with a background, avoid sudden movements, and indeed as much movement as you can. Put up the rod and make all preparations out of the fish's field of vision.

All this particularly concerns the angler seeking to deceive fish swimming near the surface in clear water, but its importance is underestimated by many 'bottom' fishermen. Every movement of a man sitting on a high bank with his rod being waved over the water may be obvious and alarming to fish many yards away. I have heard an angler argue that he could not possibly be seen by a fish near his bait yards away and feet down in the water. Possibly he was right, but he might frighten fish near him and these, darting off, would communicate their alarm to others who had seen nothing.

Another point easily overlooked is that the angler looking down into water against a dark background (the bottom) is in a very different position from a fish looking up into light from the sky. Anything outside the water is likely to be silhouetted and the silhouette does not have to be identified to cause alarm. At the same time, the movement will cause alarm only if it is unnatural. When the water is rippled, the many and constantly varying angles at which light from objects on the bank strikes the water must make them all appear to be moving. Amongst all this movement, the angler is much less likely to cause alarm and hence it is easier to fish disturbed water unobserved.

Fish living in public park ponds, or anywhere people are a commonplace presence, soon get used to living alongside such activity; and fish lying beneath road and railway bridges have to put up with massive vibrations—if they didn't they would never venture from their hiding places. Needless to say, the angler need not worry too much about stealth in such spots.

The survival of a fish depends on its ability to notice and act on danger signals, whether on the bank or in the water, like the flash of a feeding pike. Hence big fish are always likely to be shy fish. It is their shyness which has enabled them to survive long enough to grow larger than average. If you never worry about the fish's point of view you may still catch some fish, but they will generally be small ones. If you hope to deceive the larger ones, you must give as much thought to how and what fish see as to the choice of tackle and baits. An alarmed or suspicious fish is concerned only with preserving its life. However attractive the bait or lure, and however skilfully it is presented, it will not tempt the fish, even if it sees it.

2

Food for Fishes

SUCCESS in angling is completely dependent on fish being hungry. I should, perhaps, except salmon and the occasional trout or pike which seems to pursue other fish at times more because its hunting instinct is aroused by their movement than because they need food at the moment. But unless a fish can be persuaded to seize what it takes to be food, it cannot be caught by angling. A knowledge of the feeding habits of fish and of baits is therefore essential to success. Salmon do not feed in freshwater.

Unlike ourselves, fish do not eat at regular intervals. Searching for food is the major occupation of active fish, but for a variety of reasons they may rest from it for periods varying from a few hours to a week or longer. Recent scientific research has confirmed that all fish appear to fast for days at a time on occasions. Examination of the stomachs of netted fish have shown these fasting periods are rare in the height of summer, but the explanation of them does not seem to be simply scarcity of food or even fasting after a period of gluttony.

Fortunately for the angler, the starvation periods are not the same for all fish even of the same species, although there seems some evidence that fish of the same age group tend to fast at the same time. This may explain those times when waters known to hold good fish yield only small ones.

This kind of fasting is quite different from that of some species which hibernate. In winter carp spend long periods in semi-hibernation and until a few years ago it was felt that to fish for them after mid-October was a waste of time.

But even in mid-winter, it has been established, carp can often be caught. The tench stops feeding about October, burying itself in the mud until a warm spell in February or March starts it feeding again. The barbel's winter sleep which begins in November is not so profound and it may move and feed on warmer days during the winter. The habits of these fish impose a respite for them quite apart from the legal close season designed to protect them during the breeding period.

The most important factor in the day-to-day feeding activity of fish is probably the temperature of the water. Although fish do not feel heat and cold in the same way as we do, they are very sensitive to changes in temperature. Laboratory experiments have shown fish reacting to differences in temperature of as little as half a degree. The temperature of the water is therefore of great importance to the angler who is interested only in fish willing to feed. He has to bear in mind that shallows heat up and cool down more rapidly than deeps, but that in still water in winter the warmest water may be deep on the side towards which the wind is blowing because water reaches its maximum specific gravity at about forty degrees.

Experience has shown that, hibernation apart, there are minimum temperatures below which fish will not feed, at any rate enthusiastically enough to interest the angler. These temperatures vary for different species. Bream and rudd appear to stop feeding when the temperature drops below 45°, carp when the temperature is about 55°, though recent experiences by winter carp fishers would seem to question this figure. Most species appear to stop feeding when the temperature rises above 70°, but this water temperature is normally found only in the middle of summer days in still or comparatively still waters. Published observations of an angler who recorded water temperature and wind direction each time he fished for bream through one season show an apparently significant relationship between the exact temperature and the feeding activity of the fish, between 60 and 70 degrees. Wind direction is important as it results in the surface being cooled in one part faster than in the other.

A change in temperature may be as important as the absolute temperature in its effect on feeding activity. The roach feeds through a very wide range of water temperatures. But a fall below 40 degrees in winter usually results in blank days for the angler. When the temperature has persisted for some time, however, roach start feeding again.

There is a fascinating field for research here for any angler who systematically records air and water temperatures over a long period. But it is rarely that a change in temperature can be isolated as the only factor. Often it is accompanied by changes in the height and colour of the water as well as the weather. How fish can be affected by changes in air pressure, we can only guess. But the tradition that, for instance, an east wind means poor sport is a very old one and experience suggests it is well founded. The air temperature and conditions are obviously of importance to the dry-fly fisherman because he is seeking fish feeding on air-borne insects.

The weather and the water temperatures may be decisive in deciding how and where we fish for what species. But I have never allowed myself to be persuaded that the thermometer and barometer should decided whether it is worth going fishing. Blank days have been compensated for by others when good results have shown that optimism and persistence sometimes triumph over science and experience.

Systematic examination of the stomach contents of thousands of fish of different species have given us a good knowledge of their natural foods at different periods of the year. These run all the way from scarcely visible diatoms, through plants and algae, crustaceans such as water shrimps and crayfish, molluscs and insects in great variety, to other fish.

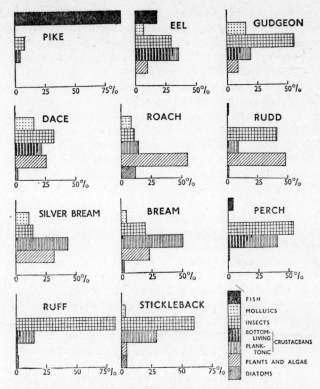

Fig. 1. Chart showing the percentage composition of the diets of some coarse fish. (From the *Interim Report on the Coarse Fish Investigation* by P. H. T. Hartley, B.Sc., by courtesy of the Freshwater Biological Association of the British Empire)

No fish restricts itself to one food, and the majority at some time feed on most of them.

But, except for small fish, very few of these natural foods are any use to the angler because they are unsuitable for impaling on a hook. He may offer artificial imitations of natural foods in the case of flies and nymphs, but generally his baits are foods which the fish would rarely, if ever, find naturally. Floods may occasionally result in a lobworm getting into a river naturally, but generally a fish is unlikely to see one except on an angler's hook. The angler's baits are all substitutes for natural foods and it is really remarkable that they are taken so readily, especially as they, generally, do not imitate the form of natural foods. We may think of a land maggot as a substitute for water molluscs and shrimps, and it has been suggested fish mistake hemp seed for small water-snails, but most baits bear little resemblance in appearance or texture to the foods which the fish are seeking.

From this I deduce that although the choice of bait is only one of many factors contributing to success, it may often be the decisive one. When fish are 'on the feed', they often appear to take any one of a wide range of baits with equal zest. But those days are exceptional and, generally, if one bait fails to produce results, it pays to try others of contrasting form and type.

The importance of different types of natural food varies both with the seasons and the size of the fish. Plants and algae are the most important food of the roach at all times and at all ages, but, presumably because they are more readily available, a higher proportion of molluscs and insects are eaten from July–August to March. And the larger the roach, the higher the proportion of animal as against vegetable foods in its diet. The fly-fisherman observes what natural food trout are taking before deciding which fly to use. The bottom angler cannot normally see fish feeding and must guess intelligently. Ringing the changes on baits of different types and sizes is logical. It may also be profitable to change the bait if a fish is struck and missed and the bites stop coming. The suspicion or alarm aroused by the old bait may not attach to a new one of another type.

In deciding on the right bait, you have to consider the species of fish, the type of water, the technique you are using and even the size of the fish. Big baits for big fish is a

fairly true generality. A change of bait can be made to avoid
unwanted fish. For instance, if you are plagued by eels when
fishing for roach or chub, a change to a vegetarian bait will
result in the eels ignoring you.

Most species of fish will take a considerable range of baits,
even if they generally show preference for two or three. I
will mention the most likely for each species in due course.
Most anglers stick to half a dozen favourites which will
cover all fish pretty well, although hardly a week passes
without a report of a good fish being taken on an unusual
bait. Experiments are always worth trying, but generally
these cases are the exceptions which prove the rule.

The only natural vegetable food from the water it is
practical to use as bait is the silkweed which grows on the
aprons of weirs. In summer fish eat this weed not merely
for its vegetable content, but also for the countless minute
animals it harbours. Fished in the water below, it can be
deadly on occasions for roach and chub. Bait by drawing
your hook several times through the weed as it lies on the
apron until you have caught up enough to conceal the hook.

The angler's common substitutes for the organic particles and plant life which form a large part of the diet of
fish which are primarily vegetarian—because their form and
teeth are not equipped to deal with other fish—are made
from flour in some form. These vegetarian baits are useless
for game fish, perch and pike, whose natural food is almost
wholly animal. But the fish which are largely vegetarian will
take animal baits.

Paste at its simplest is made by mixing stale bread crumb
and water until it is of a consistency that makes it possible
to mould it on the hook. Or you can take a piece of crumb
straight from the inside of a new loaf and work it between
finger and thumb until it is of the right consistency, which
should not be so stiff that there will be difficulty in the point
of the hook pushing through it nor so soft that it floats off
as soon as it is dropped in the water. Another way to make

paste is to cut the crust from part of a loaf, place it in a piece of clean cloth, fold over, dip in water and then squeeze hard and work until it is the right consistency. Make sure your hands are clean and avoid contamination of tobacco. Mixing a small amount of well-shredded cotton wool in the paste helps to keep the bait on the hook, but it may obstruct immediate penetration of the barb and there is the possibility it will arouse caution so that the bait is taken less boldly.

There are endless variations of this straightforward paste. You can use honey to sweeten it. You can stain it various colours with dyes sold specially for the purpose. You can try dipping the hook-bait in dry flour, blancmange or custard powder just before casting. The idea is that the fine particles on the surface will float off and make an attractive 'cloud' round the bait. This would be very quickly lost in moving water, but is worth trying in canals and lakes. You can mix the custard powder into the paste to colour it yellow. I read of a large roach taken on a paste to which a little 'tonic' made for aquarium fish had been added! All this offers possibilities for interesting experiments and there are a number of proprietary ready-mixed pastes on sale. But I do not know of any real evidence that any of the variations are consistently more successful than straightforward paste.

An alternative to paste is crust. The standard method of preparation is to cut off the crust of a loaf, put it in a damp cloth and place it under a heavy weight overnight. With the right loaf, I have found it equally good and much less trouble to use the crust cut straight from the loaf. You must bear in mind that as it floats in the water, the crust will expand considerably. The size of the piece used depends on the fish and will vary from a quarter-inch cube for shy roach to a two-inch slab for big carp.

The floating property of crust as compared with paste can be valuable in fishing over weed. Paste may sink down into the weed and become invisible to the fish. A piece of crust will rest lightly on top of the weed. You can use half-and-half, putting on a small piece of crust first and then moulding paste round the hook. This also has the advantage of keeping the crust on more securely.

Macaroni and spaghetti are basically the same type of bait, specially favoured in this form for chub. Prepare macaroni by cooking it very gently in milk until it is soft enough to go on the hook, but not so soft as you would expect if eating it yourself. It is probably most effectively fished on a treble hook, in which case you pass the hook-length through the tube and let the piece of macaroni cover the shank while it rests on the bends of the hook. Cook spaghetti in the same way and fish it on a single hook, either a little square impaled or a piece an inch or more long through one end of which you pass the hook twice, leaving a 'tail' to hang down. These pasta come in all sorts of shapes and calibres from which you can select the one most suitable to your purpose. There is a green spaghetti which looks promising but has never brought me the results I have hoped for.

The alternative type of vegetarian bait is the whole grain of a cereal, and it is probably the difference in shape rather than taste which counts. Grains of wheat are prepared by simmering them very gently, making sure they never boil, until the husk just bursts. Pearl barley is cooked until it is just soft. These grains are generally available ready prepared in tins or bottles and, unless you are going to use large quantities, buying them like this saves trouble.

Hemp seed is cooked in the same way, but because of the hardness of its husk it should be soaked first for some hours. There was much furore and controversy when this bait was first introduced. Because it proved so effective on occasions it was dubbed 'unsporting' and, perhaps through unconscious association with Indian hemp, many people believed that it drugged fish and even killed them. The result was a ban on it on many waters and this remains, although research and experience have suggested that it does not have the dire effects supposed and that it is not always effective. Many anglers will confirm that baiting with hemp seed does not make a keep-net full of roach a certainty and, taking one occasion with another, it is probably just another bait.

These grains are placed on the hook by pushing the point into the germ where it is showing and just bringing it through the husk on the other side. This must be done delicately to avoid breaking up the grain.

Cooked peas—fresh, frozen or tinned—are sometimes a good vegetable bait, and so is a piece of potato, specially favoured for carp. The potato should only be par-boiled, otherwise it will break off the hook easily. A small new potato is generally prescribed, but there is no special virtue in the newness and the idea probably originated because potatoes of a size suitable for carp, during the period when fishing for it is at its best, are new ones. A piece of old potato cut to shape is equally satisfactory. The potato must be put on the hook, a large single one or smaller treble, by using a baiting needle, the hook length being carried through the potato and pulled gently until the potato is well seated on the hook bend or bends. Leaving a small piece of skin on the potato will assist in keeping it on the hook. The bend of the hook is drawn back against the patch of skin, and by doing this it is possible to fish with potatoes cooked until they are soft enough for human consumption.

Where bushes and trees overhang the water, fish may be accustomed to feeding on fruit or insects which fall from them. In September and October, elderberries and black-berries are sometimes good baits, especially for chub, which favour water under trees, and I have known roach taken on cherries.

Cheese, alone or mixed with bread paste or flour, is an excellent bait. Chub are particularly vulnerable to the aroma of cheese, but barbel, carp, roach, dace . . . and eels! all like it too. Grated Cheddar kneaded with bread paste does well; cubes of Edam are also used widely; and Camembert, Danish blue and similar strong-smelling cheeses, often mixed with a little dry flour into a soft consistency, are other favourites. Cheeses harden in the cold water of winter, so make sure your bait is soft, else the hook will not pull through on the strike.

The bait generally used by a boy going on his first fishing expedition is a worm. His instinct is right in that the worm is the bait taken by the widest range of fish of all sizes and species. In fact there is no freshwater fish, from the lordly salmon down to the tiny bleak, that will not take a worm on occasions, and if you had no idea of what fish a piece of water contained, a worm would be the safest bait.

Worms are of many types and sizes from the fat six-inch lobworm down to the little pink worm that can be impaled only on the smallest hook. The choice will depend on the size and variety of fish expected. The essentials are that the worm should be clean, lively and reasonably tough. They are cleaned and toughened by allowing them to work their way several times through damp and earth-free sphagnum moss. A simple method is to remove top and bottom neatly from a can, place it on a piece of slate, concrete floor or any other smooth surface and fill with damp, clean moss. Put the worms on top and cover with a piece of sacking. In a few hours they will have worked their way through to the bottom. Turn the tin upside down so that they are again on top, cover and repeat several times. So long as you keep them cool and damp, but not wet, the worms will remain lively for some days. When a worm on the hook becomes drowned and lifeless, it should be replaced immediately.

FIG. 2. A worm on a two-hook Pennel tackle

To keep a worm well stretched out on

31

FIG. 3. How to put two gentles on a hook

the hook with a minimum of injury, use a hook specially made with the end of the shank turned outwards for a small fraction of an inch. After threading on the worm, draw its head up over the end of the shank which will then protrude and prevent it slipping. In fishing fast water for trout, you use a tackle in which two or even three small hooks are whipped above each other on the nylon, each being pushed once through the worm. This makes it possible to strike immediately a touch from a fish is felt.

The most widely used bait for coarse fish is probably the maggot or gentle, the larva of the ordinary blue-bottle. You can produce your own by allowing meat or fish to become 'blown' in the summer, but this is an unpleasant business and nothing but being marooned on a desert island would persuade me to do it now that gentles are so easily obtainable from commercial establishments where they are bred by the million.

Gentles are used singly on a small hook or in bunches. Push the point of the hook just through the skin under the tail, doing the smallest possible amount of damage, and allow the gentle to hang down. Only if you are using three or more is it necessary to thread them on the shank. In this case, leave at least two to hang down attractively.

The angler who is prepared to hunt for his own baits can find others which are very attractive on occasions. The only practical ones from the water itself are crayfish and caddis. In rivers containing them, crayfish can be caught in a net trap baited with something pungent like kipper, or hunted under stones in the shallows. Pass the hook right through the tail so that it hangs downwards. You find the caddis in the shallows of clean streams, camouflaged with a sheath covered in tiny bits of stone or sticks to match the bottom. Its head protrudes from one end and you

3. The completion of an Avon cast

4. Good netting technique. The beaten chub has been brought over the net which the angler is drawing towards him before lifting. The head of the fish has been lifted more than necessary for the sake of clarity

5. Spinning with a fixed-spool reel in the upper Liffey. Slender as the outfit may look, it is quite capable of dealing with a salmon of twenty pounds or more

must pull it out very gently. Place it on the hook like a gentle.

If you can find and destroy a wasps' nest, you will get scores of grubs of all sizes. The larger ones are good hook-baits and the immature ones can be thrown in a few at a time as ground-bait. The one trouble is that the grubs are not as tough as gentles and baking them in a cool oven, which is recommended for toughening them, makes them less appealing.

During the summer, the angler who is a gardener will find it worth preserving caterpillars, which sometimes appeal when gentles are doing no good, especially in water under trees. If you can handle them, the earwigs collected in the flowerpots used to protect your dahlias are often good, just nicked on a very small hook. Even slugs are a good bait for the voracious chub. Thread them on the hook head downwards. The fact is, most grubs and small insects can be used as baits, including the dock grub, found at the roots of dock plants, and the grasshopper. My own experience is that the more readily obtainable worm and gentle is normally as good a bait as any for the primarily flesh-eating fish, but that there are occasions, especially during the late summer months, when one or other of these more unusual baits can be very effective.

There remains the bait of another small fish, which may range in size from a tiny minnow to a half-pound fish. They are in many conditions the most consistently effective bait for the predatory fish, especially big specimens. But many anglers do not like using them for humanitarian or, perhaps more correctly, sentimental reasons. That is something every angler has to decide for himself. In the case of trout, we do not have to use a live minnow, because a trout is fast and active enough to pursue a dead one moving rapidly. Perch and pike, although they will take a dead fish given artificial life, prefer the anchored live-bait which presents an easier meal. Large chub sometimes take a live minnow and so,

C 33

very occasionally, will a roach. The fact of the matter is that although we talk about 'cannibal' fish as if they were exceptional and unpleasant, all fish are cannibals at times, if an easy meal comes their way.

Minnows may be caught in a bread-baited trap, but roach, dace, gudgeon and bleak must be caught by angling. Many anglers now use only a hook in the live-bait's lip, though some still use a treble hook as well, nicked into the back behind the dorsal fin, or a treble in the mouth and one in the back. Since all British predatory fish swallow prey whole, the lip-hooked bait will succeed if the angler strikes at the correct time, when the head of the bait is in the fish's mouth. Always hook and cast live-baits gently, so they remain alive and lively.

All methods of angling with bait can be divided into two types. To put it crudely, either the bait is cast into the water in the hope that fish will be attracted to it, or the angler searches for fish, moving from place to place until he finds them. If the bait is to remain in the same place or a very limited area, ground-baiting is essential to produce good results. Ground-bait is food thrown into the water in the neighbourhood of the hook-bait to attract fish to the area and to keep them there. To be effective, you must use it purposefully and imaginatively. I think of ground-bait as being like the aroma which issues from the window of a restaurant and makes passers-by stop to sniff, realize they are hungry and move in through the door for a meal.

Ground-bait must attract, arouse interest and stimulate appetite without satisfying it. The standard mixtures are of well-pulped bread mixed with bran, fine chicken meal and similar material. This will break up in the water and disperse fine particles over a considerable distance. You do not want it on the surface but at the depth where the fish are normally to be found, so the bait is rolled into a ball before being thrown in. This makes it easier to throw and place and the ball will sink before it begins to disintegrate into fine pieces. The size of the ball may be varied from that of a walnut to one as big as your fist, depending on the conditions and your purpose.

Before throwing in any ground-bait work out what will happen to it after it has hit the water at the spot you have chosen. In still or almost still water, it will remain in one place and disperse slowly over a comparatively small area. If there is a current, the ball itself may be carried along the bottom and certainly the tiny fragments as they break off will travel a considerable distance straight downstream. In a deep and strong stream, you may need a big ball with a stone in its centre to carry it quickly to the bottom before it breaks up. The ground-bait will be wasted if it is dispersed by a strong current a foot or two under the surface when

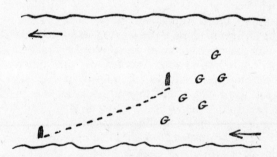

Fig. 4. How to place ground-bait. The dotted line shows the movement of float down the swim. Place ground-bait at spots marked *G*

the fish are twelve feet down. If the ball breaks up before it reaches the bottom, nine-tenths of the ground-bait is likely to be wasted as far as attracting fish to your hook-bait is concerned. On the bottom the ball will quickly be impeded by mud, stones or weeds and break up slowly into fragments that are swept along the river-bed.

In still water, small knobs of ground-bait serve the purpose much better and you would throw them to surround the area you are fishing rather than on one side of it. Here you need a ground-bait of very fine particles—'cloud-bait' aptly describes it, with minute fragments of powdered material being suspended in the water as drops of moisture are in a cloud in the sky.

A ground-bait of this kind can be made from slices of bread which have been completely dried and then finely ground or powdered. If the crust is used you get golden-coloured fragments and you can add custard powder, ground rice and similar substances to taste. More easily, you can buy ready-made cloud-baits and, as the amount you will need is comparatively small, this is not expensive.

If you are using gentles or worms as the hook-bait some of these may be incorporated in the ground-bait. Not enough to satiate the fish, but enough to get them on the look-out for more. Alternatively a few of the smallest gentles can be thrown in alone if the point at which you are fishing is within reach. Or you can use a special catapult to shoot maggots into your swim. Another way of ground-baiting with maggots, especially useful in fast water, is with a bait dropper, which you attach to your hook, fill with maggots, then cast into your swim. On touching bottom, a door on the dropper opens, spilling maggots onto the river-bed. This prevents wastage, where hand-introduced maggots would be swept away downstream by the fast upper current. It has been much argued about how necessary it is to have ground-bait and hook-bait related. A bread and bran or cloud ground-bait can be effective even if your hook-bait is a gentle or worm. But in the case of some baits there seems little doubt ground-baiting is necessary to 'educate' the fish as well as attract them. If you use peas on the hook, there should be some well-broken-up ones in the ground-bait. A carp that has never come across a boiled potato before may not immediately realize it is good eating and pass by. But if potatoes have been lying about in the spots the carp frequents for several days, it has probably sampled them, found them good and is ready to appreciate the one on the angler's hook.

Out of necessity most anglers can use ground-bait only immediately before they begin fishing. But, especially for fish which roam in search of food, it pays if possible to ground-bait the evening before and, in some cases, systematically for some days before so that the fish have come to expect food in that particular spot.

The interest of the fish being aroused, you want to keep them round your hook-bait, more interested in food than in the disturbance that has been created by your hooking and landing a fish. You continue to use ground-bait during the whole period you are fishing, but judiciously, bearing in mind that its purpose is to attract and interest the fish and not to feed them. I suspect that the danger of over-ground-baiting is exaggerated, at any rate in well-stocked waters, and that in fact most anglers underestimate the amount of ground-bait required. It is impossible to generalize for all waters and all kinds of fish, but seven pounds of ground-bait would be none too much for a day's fishing on many waters. On a deep and strong river like the Hampshire Avon, which has a big fish population and where much of the ground-bait is likely to be 'wasted', you could in many places use as much ground-bait as you could carry without any danger of satiating the fish.

Ground-bait of the usual type is obviously of little use when you are after fish which are uninterested in vegetable foods, such as perch, pike and trout. I have known cloud ground-bait used round a live-bait for pike on the theory that it would attract small fish which, in turn, would attract pike. Worms can be used as ground-bait by rolling them into a ball of clay which is slowly washed away on the bottom, releasing the worms one by one, but this form of ground-baiting is normally used only for barbel.

Generally, in angling for the predatory fish, we seek out the fish rather than try to gather them round a bait in a limited area. This may be done with one of the 'animal' baits or by using a completely inedible imitation of a natural bait, relying on its appearance to deceive long enough for the fish to take it into its mouth. They obviously have to be kept moving to have any chance of success and will be dealt with more conveniently in the chapters on fly-fishing and spinning.

3

Choosing and Using Tackle

I AM sure there are thousands of anglers who like myself find turning over the pages of catalogues or looking round a tackle shop almost as fascinating as fishing. What wonderful catches we make in imagination as we examine the rods, reels, floats, flies, spinners and all the rest of that tremendous range of tackle now available! We may know at the bottom of our hearts that when it comes to the point we should do just as well with the tackle that has served so well in the past, but adding to the collection is almost irresistible and I sympathize with anglers who make the collection of tackle almost a hobby in its own right apart from fishing.

In recent years so many new techniques of angling have been evolved to catch the increasingly difficult-to-fool quarry, that the freshwater angler with at least ten rods is not now considered to be a 'collector'. But one needs to be a very competent and knowledgeable angler to appreciate the need for a very wide range of rods, reels, etc., and when in the initial stages of learning about the art one needs to know more of the real essentials rather than the refinements—such as a special rod for hooking carp at ranges of seventy yards—in order to be able to afford the tools of the trade without risking the debtors' court!

Here rods and tackle must be dealt with not as objects to stimulate daydreams but strictly from the utilitarian point of view. The sole purpose of all tackle is to place a natural or artificial bait in the right position and then to hook the fish and bring it to the bank. The efficiency of the whole outfit in performing these tasks must decide the selection of the individual parts.

The Rod

A rod serves a number or purposes. As a combination of lever and spring it helps to get the bait or lure to the desired position. It makes it easier to impart to the line the sudden movement which drives home the hook quickly. When a fish is hooked, its springiness provides a cushion against sudden strains which might otherwise break the line. These different purposes call for qualities which are, to some extent, incompatible, and every rod is, therefore, something of a compromise. For instance, the float-fisherman may demand a rod which responds immediately when he strikes, but this must to some extent reduce the efficiency of the rod in casting.

Ninety percent of today's rods are made from hollow glass-fibre and split cane (bamboo) is now used rarely for anything but fly rods, for which the wood is supreme in many contexts. So advanced is the production of hollow glass blanks for rods that it is commonplace to find a rod suitable for catching (say) dace and roach on the one hand, yet be fine for twenty-pound carp on the other, about eleven feet in length and weighing a mere seven ounces. The tapers can be mathematically worked out and each rod kept to an identical specification.

Ideally there would be just one rod that was perfect for dealing with a particular size or class of fish and technique of angling. The cost apart, equipment with such an armoury is obviously impractical for the all-round angler. Unless you are going to restrict yourself to one type of water and one technique, you must be prepared for compromise. The one compromise that is impossible is a rod that will cast a fly, a spinning bait and a float. The qualities required for each of these forms of fishing are so different that any attempt at building a rod combining them would only result in one unsatisfactory for any of them. The 'combination rod' in which joints are interchangeable to produce a number of different rods of varying lengths and stiffness is not altogether satisfactory. Although a rod is made in two or three pieces for convenience in transport, it should be designed as a single unit.

But the all-round angler who chooses rightly three rods, primarily designed for bottom-fishing, spinning and fly-fishing, can be confident that he is equipped to catch any kind of freshwater fish in any kind of water without being unduly handicapped. The choice of a rod for fly-fishing I will deal with in the chapter devoted to that subject. If the spinning-rod is also to do service as a pike rod and possibly as a light sea-rod you want a fairly heavy one of about eight foot. This may seem rather clumsy for catching trout of a pound or two, but then a light rod suitable for this would be put to undue strain in handling big pike or carp, so we have to compromise.

For bottom-fishing you require a rod that will throw an ounce weight ten or fifteen yards, respond instantly to the strike you make in response to a touch from a half-pound roach and yet enable you to play a three- or four-pound chub if you hook one. The range of rods designed to meet these requirements is now enormous and likely to be bewildering to the beginner. The one most likely to be satisfactory in the widest range of conditions is probably an Avon type rod of ten or eleven feet. If you choose one by a first-class maker it will have stand-off rod-rings making for an easy-running line that will not stick to the rod when it is wet. My overriding advice is to remember that a rod is a long-term investment. Properly cared for it will last for many years. A good rod is a thing of beauty and a work of art. It cannot be cheap. A cheap rod cannot be a good one, although that does not mean all expensive rods are good ones. If you have not an expert friend to help you choose,

41

put your faith in a good tackle shop and insist on a rod by one of the famous makers. You must expect to pay twelve to twenty pounds, but divide that by the number of years you will use it and it will seem cheap! Your spinning-rod will be a two-piece. Your 'bottom rod' will be either two- or three-piece.

A great deal of expense may be saved on rods today because of the general use of hollow glass-fibre. Many tackle shops, some of which specialize, can supply the blanks and all the bits and pieces from which you can make your own rods at very nearly half the price of the finished factory-made job. Do not be put off because you feel ham-fisted and that the job is too much for your capabilities. The blanks can be bought ready fitted with joints or glass-to-glass spigots, which are better, and cork handles, shaped and bored ready to glue on, plus reel fittings and the suitable rings.

A child of ten years with reasonable intelligence can make a good rod today from a kit. With patience and care, whipping on rings, fixing fittings with modern adhesives and finally finishing the whole rod with a couple of coats of varnish can result in a 'first home-made rod' to be proud of. Two or three evenings or a weekend will see the job done, and catching fish on a rod made at home is extremely pleasurable as well as cheap.

The Reel

Reels fall into three broad classes. The centre-pin reel consists essentially of a wooden or metal drum which revolves smoothly, but can be braked by a check. The handle of the reel revolves with it and the amount of line paid out or taken in with each revolution will depend on the diameter of the reel. The multiplier is made of metal and the handle geared so that one turn produces several revolutions of the drum. The reel sometimes has a free-spool system so that the drum can spin freely without the handle revolving, thus offering a minimum resistance to line being drawn off.

42

Then there are the fixed-spool reels which have grown so rapidly in popularity since the war. Here the drum has its axis parallel with the rod instead of at right angles to it as in other types. As its name implies, the drum does not revolve. Line is drawn directly from it and wound back onto it by means of a revolving arm geared to the handle.

There is an enormous choice within these categories, both in size and mechanical refinements. Each of the different types has advantages and disadvantages for various angling techniques. With a centre pin you are, so to speak, in direct contact with the fish. With a suitable centre pin you can practise almost every method of angling. Its disadvantage from the point of view of the beginner is that learning to control it when casting requires considerable practice.

The multiplier's advantages are that, thanks to the free-spool system, the drum revolves freely enough to cast a light weight and that the gearing makes quick recovery possible. Especially if the reel is fitted with a device to prevent it overrunning, it is much easier to learn to cast with it. Small freshwater multipliers, some of which have star-drag systems as well as free-spool systems, are excellent for pike and salmon spinning, or for pike live- and dead-baiting. Lines of about eight pounds breaking strain and upwards are in general use. The larger saltwater multiplier is the most popular type of reel among sea-anglers, both for shore fishing and boat fishing.

The advantage of the fixed-spool reel is that there is a minimum of resistance to line being drawn off so that it can be used to cast very light weights such as a small float with a single shot. If it is not quite so foolproof as it may seem, you can learn to cast long distances with it in less than an hour. Its disadvantage is perhaps that it does not give the same control of a hooked fish. If you must be content with a single reel, the best choice would probably be a fixed-spool which can be used for almost every technique except casting a fly. But a better decision if possible would be to have a

43

centre-pin reel for your bottom rod and a fixed-spool reel for spinning.

Choose a caged pin reel of four to five inches. A reel with a small diameter will not give sufficiently quick recovery if you have to deal with a strong fish and will not allow you to long trot, a technique almost essential for success on some rivers. You can get usable pin reels for a pound or two, but as with the rod it pays to buy one by a well-known maker for perhaps three times as much.

The boom in fixed-spool reels has resulted in the appearance of a bewildering number of types, most of them good, some not so good, with the price not necessarily indicating the order of merit. A first-class reel by a good maker may cost you eight to ten pounds, but it is only right to say there are fixed-spool reels at half this price which are perfectly serviceable and capable of having a long life if cared for.

As you will be using this reel for spinning and heavy fish, select one of a size that will hold at least 100 yards of line of six pounds breaking strength. It is an advantage to have one with interchangeable spools which can be filled with lines of different strengths. A good fixed-spool reel is a fine piece of mechanism and should have the routine care advised by the maker.

In water a fish is virtually weightless, which explains why it is possible to bring to the bank a fish weighing, say, four pounds on a line with a breaking strength of only half that weight. Once the fish is lifted out of the water, its whole weight is exerted. At the same time it is likely to wriggle violently, tearing away the hook-hold. For this reason, instead of trying to lift it out of the water on to the bank, we draw it over a net so that its weight is supported. The essential of your landing-net is that it should have an opening much wider than the largest fish you hope to catch, so that the fish can be brought over it easily. The net may look a little ridiculous when you are catching half-pounders, but you will be glad of it when you do get a big fish. A long handle is a great advantage except when you are continually on the move, as in spinning and fly-fishing, when it is an encumbrance. Then you need a net that can be slung on your back or a folding one which clips to your belt. Some anglers object to the folding-net on the ground that it always seems to stick and refuse to unfold at the critical moment, but this should not really be a trouble if it is well designed and made and the joint kept oiled. You can carry your long-handled net, putting it down to leave your hands free every time you cast, but apart from being tiresome this always ends up sooner or later with your bringing a good fish in only to find you forgot to pick up your net the last time you moved on. In this situation you can often save your fish by playing it right out and finding a suitable place to beach it, drawing it from gently shelving water to dry land.

The Hook

Hooks are made in all sizes from the minute Nos. 18 and 20, favoured by match anglers who are after fish regardless of size, down to No. 3 which is about the largest likely to be used by the freshwater angler. Your choice of size will depend on the nature and size of the bait and the size of the fish expected. You cannot put a worm on a No. 18 hook nor expect it to hold a four-pound chub. On the other hand, a single gentle would look foolish on a No. 6 hook, apart from the fact that it would probably be killed instantly by the attempt to impale it. There is some margin of choice between these extremes and, if the fish seem shy, you may start with a hook which is on the small side and change to a bigger one as soon as the fish begin biting well.

If you carry a selection of hooks, from size 3 down to size 16, you will be ready for everything, from pike to minnows. I suggest ringed hooks, which may be tied to nylon monofilament or twisted to wire (for live-baiting for pike, etc.). Alternatively choose spade-end hooks to whip to nylon

45

(sizes 16 to 8), and carry ringed sizes 6 to 3, which can be tied on to nylon or twisted to wire.

Hooks are made in numerous shapes with many different finishes—blued, bronzed, nickel plated, gilt plated—from tempered steel wire. Some are made from stainless steel wire, others from monel metal, an alloy.

In some, the wire is uniformly round, in others flattened on the bend. The latter are termed 'forged' and the strongest type. To attach them to the line the ends of the shanks may be fashioned with an eye, turned up or down, with a small straight eye in line with the shanked (these are 'ringed' hooks), with a flattened end (spade end), or have the shanks serrated so that the nylon may be whipped to them and thus have a key against the steel.

In some the point is in line with the shank while in others the hook is offset to right or left when viewed from the shank side towards the point, which is said to improve its hooking power. Shank lengths also vary, but in general a medium shank length is desirable.

Whatever type you buy, it is never worth saving a shilling or two a dozen at the risk of one day losing the fish of your lifetime.

The Float

There is now an immense range of floats in many materials and colours. Half a dozen floats of different types and sizes will cover most conditions, but floats are comparatively cheap and rarely lost, so that building up a collection is not expensive. A float is used for two purposes. It enables you to keep your bait at any depth you wish from just touching the bottom to within a foot of the surface and to have it carried by the current at this constant depth. At the same time it acts as a signal, telling of any interference with the bait. The signals vary from complete disappearance under the surface in a fraction of a second, showing the bait is being carried away, to falling flat on the surface, showing the bait is being lifted. Between these extremes there are an infinite variety of signals from a barely perceptible quiver to a slight change in the angle made with the surface. Although it is possible to generalize about the ways different fish take a bait as indicated by the movements of a float, only experience and imagination will result in an angler always interpreting the signals in terms of the position of his hook in relation to the mouth of the fish so that he can drive home the barb at the correct moment.

Every float requires a certain definite weight to make it cock and float upright. But the right approach to picking a float for a particular occasion is to decide first the weight necessary on your cast to carry the bait where and as you want it and then pick a float that matches the weight. Fishing a deep-swim river with a strong current, you need sufficient weight to take the bait down quickly, otherwise the float will sail in advance, towing the weight unnaturally and perhaps reaching the limit of the swim before the bait is on the bottom. Equally deep still water calls for much less weight and can be fished with a much lighter float. For the heavier water you would use a quill given additional buoyancy by being cased in cork or balsa wood, or expanded polystyrene for most of its length. For the still water a small quill meets the case.

But the distance a tiny quill and cast with one or two shots can be cast is limited, especially against a breeze. A long cast might call for more weight and thus a larger float. In general, you choose a simple quill for canals and sluggish rivers and the cork-bodied 'Thames' float or the more modern balsa-wood or plastic foam Avon-type floats for the deeper swims of heavier rivers.

Special conditions call for variations of these basic types. If you are float-fishing a stream with a rocky bottom, which will generally be for grayling, you avoid the crazy motions the uneven current would give a tapered float by using a pilot float, a little cork sphere. Where the depth to be fished is considerable, a float fixed to the line causes trouble in casting and when you reel in you find the float obstructing the top ring of your rod before you have your bait or fish out of water. The answer is to use a sliding float, the essential difference of which is that it is fitted with wire rings at top and bottom through which the line can slide freely until it meets an obstruction.

A shot, tiny piece of rubber or very short piece of nylon which will pass easily through the rod-rings but not through the top ring of the float is tied at the depth selected for fishing. When you lift your line, the float slides down until its lower ring is obstructed by the top shot on your cast, perhaps two feet from the hook. In this position it can be cast easily. Immediately it hits the water, the weights pull the line through the rings of the float until the 'stop' you have tied obstructs the top ring. The bait now is at the depth you require, perhaps twelve or twenty feet, and the float is as sensitive as an ordinary one. When you reel in, the float slides down the line until it is stopped by the shot.

Gusty winds and choppy water make the float lean and rock so that detecting bites is difficult. The float gets blown over the water and the bait below may be moved in an unnatural way. The antennae float is designed to meet these conditions by being made so that its centre of gravity is well below the surface and only the tip is exposed to wind and waves. Alternatively you can use a small quill, fixed to your line only at its bottom end, the usual

Fig. 5. Thames-type sliding float

48

6. Salmon and scenery. The angler is promised a battle if she hooks a fish in this strong water and it runs downstream below her

7. Irish sea angling can be superb: a bass on light tackle in the Kerry surf

rubber band for fixing to the top being left off.

As far as the submerged part of a float is concerned, colour is probably of no importance so long as it more or less blends with the water. It may be an advantage in the case of a substantial float not to have it too highly polished, so that there is no chance of it producing flashes which could be seen by fish far below. When using the antenna float or the bottom-attached long quill, it is, of course, necessary to sink the line from the float to tip of the rod by putting the rod tip under water.

The colour of the visible portion is a matter of personal choice, but most people find yellow or light orange, rather than the red favoured by some makers, gives better visibility at a distance. In a poor light, a float treated with the fluorescent paint now available has advantages. A float to the top of which caps of different colours can be fitted gives a wide choice for different conditions without the trouble of having to change the whole float. Watching a float at a considerable distance in a poor

FIG. 6. Antenna float for use in wind

light can be trying. If you slice a thin disc from a bottle cork and slip it over the end of the float so that it is about half an inch above the surface of the water, any movement of the float downwards will produce a ring ripple and in still water this can be easily seen at some distance.

The Line

The modern angler uses two basic materials for his lines:

D   49

nylon and terylene. Most fishing is carried out with mono-filament nylon, which is the liquid material extruded through various calibrated nozzles, then set. It is used for most types of coarse fishing, for spinning and for salt-water fishing.

Nylon braided lines are also used to a limited extent, mainly for spinning and live- and dead-baiting for pike. Braided terylene is more popular than braided nylon, because it is stronger for the same calibre and it stretches far less.

When coarse fishing, it is possible to have only one knot in the tackle—that which connects the hook to the line. In general, a tucked half-blood knot is used, although spade-end hooks are attached using a whipping knot on the hook shank.

Nylon monofilament is the cheapest line, but the price varies with quality. It is used in breaking strains from one pound up to, perhaps, sixty pounds by the sea-angler. Quoted breaking strains are frequently for the dry material. When it absorbs water nylon loses a percentage of its strength, perhaps as much as 30 per cent. It pays to bear this in mind when buying a line for a certain type of fishing. Knotting also further weakens the line, as it does any other textile material, but with the correct knots, properly tied, the loss is not great.

The greatest enemy of monofilament nylon is sunlight. So never buy line taken from a shop window, and keep your reels loaded with line out of the sun.

Four knots will suffice for monofilament nylon. For attaching hooks, flies, swivels and lures, etc., the tucked half-blood knot is best. For joining lengths of nylon (as in making up leaders for fly-fishing) two knots may be used: the four-turn blood knot, which is perfectly satisfactory for the thicker part of the leader where the breaking strain of the material may be twelve to twenty pounds, and the four-turn water knot, which is best for the thin end of the leader, which may be as little as two pounds breaking strain.

The water knot is stronger than the blood, but it takes up more material, which must be wasted. It has, however, a big attribute, which is that one end of the finished knot may be left long as a dropper on which an additional fly or flies may be tied, without much weakening of the knot.

FIG. 7. Blood knot, for joining two lengths of gut or nylon. For nylon it is made more secure if four turns are taken

FIG. 7A. Four-turn water knot—simply four overhand knots in the two pieces of nylon laid side by side. One is shown in black, the other white.

A dropper may be left on a blood knot, but the dropper is not so strong.

For making loops in monofilament, the blood bight is good.

All knots should be snugged up carefully so that turns do not overlap. Just before pulling tight, moisten the knots with saliva, which lubricates the coils and makes a better job.

Sea anglers use monofilament nylon for most of their fishing, except that for heavy common skate, conger eels, halibut, sharks, etc., braided terylene is sometimes used because it is less elastic and is less prone to contract after having great pressure applied to it, as does monofilament, and so crush the spools of the reel.

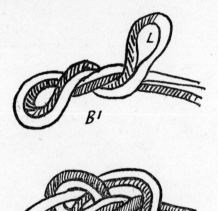

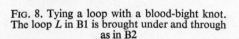

FIG. 8. Tying a loop with a blood-bight knot. The loop *L* in B1 is brought under and through as in B2

Lines for fly-fishing are also made from nylon and terylene, and from silk, too, although that material is fast going out of favour. Floating fly lines are generally made from braided nylon as a core over which a plastic dressing, enclosing air bubbles, is laid. The resulting line has a specific gravity less than that of water, so it remains floating. With terylene as the core material and a plastic coating without air bubbles, a sinking line is made; sinking lines are produced which sink slowly, fast, and very fast. Terylene is heavier than nylon, of course.

The old braided silk fly lines, dressed with oil, have to be coated with a line grease to make them float, and they still sink despite this. When they do, they have to be dried and then regreased. Some anglers still use them because they are thinner for their weight than modern plastic-coated lines, and so cast better into a wind.

Some modern fly lines have floating line following a

FIG. 9. The tucked half-blood knot for attaching hook, fly, swivel, lure, etc.

final fifteen feet or so of sinking line, which makes deep fishing of flies possible without the trouble of lifting sunken line from the water to recast.

Line profiles vary, too. There are four basic shapes of line: level, double taper, weight forward, and the shooting taper, or shooting head. Level is the cheapest and is suitable for sunk-line fishing on streams and lakes. Double taper lines are thin at each end and have a thick middle section. They present a dry fly delicately. Weight-forward lines are thin at the tip, taper up to a shortish belly section, then taper off quickly again to thin line. This running line shoots easily through the rod rings and thus the weight-forward line casts farther than the double taper. The shooting taper, or head, is like the front part of the weight-forward line, but there it ends. Instead of having a continuation of thin fly line the shooting taper has a loop for attachment to a backing of monofilament nylon of between twenty and thirty pounds breaking strain. This nylon shoots through the rings better than the thin dressed line of the weight-forward line and many reservoir trout anglers use them, although they are not so effective as floating lines as they are as sinkers. And they are difficult to make alight lightly on the water.

4

Getting the Bait to the Fish

THE most effective method of bringing a bait to the notice of a fish varies with the feeding habits of the fish, the type of water to be fished and the weather conditions. There is no single right method for any particular fish or water in all conditions, but the choice should not be merely a matter of whim. An angler ought to be equipped and ready to switch from one method to another if there seems to be a reason for doing so, and the reason may be as simple as that the first has not brought results or that he wants to put down his rod and have his hands free while he eats his sandwiches.

All the techniques fall into two classes—those in which the bait remains in one place on the bottom and those in which the bait is free to move in the water. If the bait is to be free, a float is normally required. One exception is in clear-water worm-fishing for trout. This is a special art of its own requiring a considerable degree of skill. It is best practised on small, rocky streams in July and August, and generally requires wading to give any chance of approach unseen by the trout in the low, clear water. The specialists use a very light rod, twelve or even fourteen feet long, of hollow glass, or with a split-cane top and whole cane below. This can be used all day without the angler becoming tired and gives the reach that is so valuable.

But you could use your bottom rod. Use a three-yard leader of two- to three-pound b.s. nylon and either a single No. 8 hook or preferably the special two-hook worm tackle I have described. On many days and waters you will require no weight at all, but if some of the water you are going to fish is both strong and deep, you will need a single shot about six inches above the hook. This also helps to swing the bait forward if there is a strong downstream wind—you always fish upstream.

Draw off sufficient line to enable you to cast forwards underhand—this will be about one and a half times the length of your rod. Now drop the worm into the stream in a likely place upstream. As soon as the worm sinks in the water it will be carried towards you by the current and you must raise your rod in time with it, so to speak, so that the line between rod tip and worm is always straight. The worm will be swept along the bottom and it takes a little experience to learn the difference between the tug of a trout attacking it and a check due to hitting a stone. A safe rule is to strike gently at the slightest check, although if you are using a single hook you should pause for two or three seconds before striking.

Success calls for silent approach, constant industry and above all 'an eye for water', picking out the likely spots to fish which in many cases will give your bait a run of only a yard or two before you have to lift it from the water to prevent getting hung up. In the kind of stream and conditions where you would use the upstream worm, you will find fish in the little eddy behind a big stone, in the water behind the tails of pools, in little 'harbours' resulting from an uneven contour of the bank—anywhere that a fish could lie head upstream without having to fight the current but able to see anything being brought down. It is essential that the bait travels down to it quite naturally at the speed of the current—there must be no 'drag' due to the current carrying the line down faster than the bait is moving over the bottom.

This method of fishing, which is possible only in clear, tumbling streams, is, in fact, more akin to fly-fishing than to 'bottom-fishing' as we normally think of it. The fly-rod and line which I deal with in a later chapter could be used for it

56

quite effectively with the advantage that you could cast overhead.

To attempt to use a float in such a stream would be absurd. Apart from frightening the fish in the shallow, clear water, the depth varies every few feet and your worm would sometimes be on the bottom and sometimes far off it. But in every other kind of water, you use a float if you want your bait to be free, unless you are 'free-lining', which entails drifting a bait down a river for chub, or roach, with nothing on the line but a hook, or floating a piece of breadcrust on still water for carp or rudd.

To set the float accurately, it is essential to know the exact depth of the water. You discover this by plumbing. Pass your bare hook through the loop in the plummet and push the point into the bit of cork set in the bottom of the lead. Adjust your float to the depth you guess and drop the plummet into the water you are going to fish. If the float goes under, it is too low. If it lies flat, it is too high. Adjust it accordingly until you have the exact depth.

In still water you will normally need only one or two shot nine to twelve inches from the hook to carry the bait down and these will call for the lightest quill float. Sometimes in summer fish are seeking food in a zone several feet in depth and not merely on or near the bottom. If you put your shots only a few inches below the float, they will let the bait fall slowly through the feeding zone. Or you can use a self-cocking float which requires no shot on the line. Wrapping the necessary weight of lead wire round the bottom of an ordinary float will make it self-cocking. With this falling bait, you must strike at the slightest suggestion of interference. When casting in still water, I try to get the line below the float to fall straight on the water so that there is little or no slack as the bait sinks until it is right under the float.

This method is useful when fishing over a bottom heavily covered with weed. If you have shot near the bait, they will carry the bait to the bottom with the probability that it becomes hidden and covered in weed. Fish with the shot well up and the bait will fall so lightly that it will rest on or among the weeds and be visible and clean.

Short casts of little more than a rod's length present no difficulty with even the lightest tackle. For longer casts there are two standard techniques both of which take some practice to master. To learn to cast in the Nottingham style, take a loop of line from between butt and the next ring up on your rod with your left hand, drawing line off your reel to bring the loop right down. Make your cast and, as the line swings forwards over the water, release the loop held in your left hand. It will be drawn through the top ring and the length of your cast will be increased by the length of the loop.

When you have mastered the timing of this, you can take an additional loop from the section above the first. This must be released just as the first loop is running through and will be drawn after it. An angler skilled in this style can manage three or even four loops, each being released in turn at exactly the right moment.

The Avon style of casting requires a free-running centre-pin reel. Lower the float from the rod point until you have a comfortable length for casting, about three-quarters the length of your rod. Hold your cast between the third and fourth fingers of your left hand. Catch the line as it comes from the reel with your left thumb, at the same time putting your right finger on the reel to prevent it turning. Now comes the difficult movement. You cast by swinging the rod and at the same time draw your left hand away quickly so that the line over your thumb overcomes the inertia of the reel and starts it moving. Release the cast at the correct moment and it flies out, drawing line from the reel. At the moment it begins to fall your right finger on the reel begins to check it to prevent overrunning. A more modern form involves flicking the reel into motion with the finger or thumb of the hand holding the rod as an overhead cast is made. The spinning drum of the reel is controlled with the same finger or thumb.

If all goes well, your float is now riding twenty yards away. But it is only right to say that while casting like this may look easy when it is done by a skilled angler, mastery requires as much, and perhaps, more skill and practice than a twenty-yard cast of a dry fly. The fixed-spool reel makes it possible to cast direct from the reel, even with a very light weight, without the complication of having to overcome inertia or serious danger of overrunning, the technique being the same as that for spinning described in a later chapter.

When fishing still water, you need only sufficient weight to enable you to cast and to carry your bait to the bottom. When there is a current, you need shot near the bait to prevent the bait streaming out behind as the float is carried downstream. The exact arrangement of the weights will affect the behaviour of the bait once it is in the water and you should try to visualize this in deciding where to place them. A single heavy weight or group of shot near the bait will carry it straight down. But a fish is likely to feel a check as soon as it touches the bait. If the shot are distributed widely over the nylon, the bait will not fall so fast, but there will be less resistance when a fish touches it. Whether and how you concentrate your shot or spread them must depend on the exact circumstances, and should never be a matter of chance. If fish are shy or on the small side, it is probably better to have the greater part of the weight well back from the bait.

You can float-fish moving water either by swimming the stream or by long trotting. Swimming the stream is quite straightforward. You cast to the upstream end of your swim and as the current carries your float down, you follow it with your rod until it is checked at the limit of your line when you draw in and cast again. Sometimes it pays to hold the float back for a minute at the end of its journey, so that the bait, carried on by the current, rises and streams out. But generally, the object should be to have the bait tripping along or just above the bottom at the natural speed of the current.

Where the water is suitable, long trotting is effective. In clear water where the fish are easily alarmed it makes it possible to fish a swim fifty yards or more away without any splashing from casting. The essential is a fairly heavy stream and a clear run for your float straight downstream. In summer this will generally be between banks of weeds. Swims of this kind which can be fished from the bank are not easy to find except where a bit of bank sticking out or some other natural feature gives you command or a run of twenty yards or more straight downstream. A boat or punt makes finding a suitable swim much easier and in this case the first essential is to master the art of drifting the boat to the head of the swim and anchoring it broadside on with a minimum of disturbance.

Apart from the need to get the bait down in the strong stream, you need plenty of weight for the sturdy float essential to exert sufficient pull to draw line from the reel which must be very free-running. Plumb the depth and set the float so that the bait will just skip along the bottom. If you are fishing from the bank, drop the float a little upstream so that by the time it is opposite you it is riding naturally with the bait well down. At this moment, give the reel a little push to start it turning. Once its inertia is overcome, it should turn quite smoothly in response to the pull of the float as it is carried downstream. If it does not, it means your float is not large enough to exert the necessary pull.

The float will ride smoothly down to the limits of the swim or your eyesight, taking the bait to fish far away. Although you may get a bite at any point, generally it will be when the float has travelled twenty yards or more. Your strike must be vigorous to deal with the length of line you have out. If a run produces no result, reel in and repeat.

If your reel does not run freely enough for the current to draw off the line, you can long trot by pulling off line from the reel with your left hand and lowering and raising the rod so that it is paid out in exact time with the current. You must not have slack line out or your strike will generally be hopelessly late in reaching the hook. On the other hand, if the float goes down by starts and stops instead of absolutely naturally at the speed of the current, the whole purpose of the method is lost. Fixed-spool reels produce this fault and so are not very suitable for trotting, specially on deep and fast rivers like the Hants Avon, Wye and Severn.

Where you want the bait anchored to one spot instead of free to move in the water there are two techniques, paternostering and ledgering. The use of the pasternoster in fresh water is usually for fishing with live-bait for perch and pike. Its advantage is that you can place the bait with considerable precision in a small area at any desired distance from the bottom. A paternoster consists essentially of a weight at the end of the line sufficient to hold the bottom with a hook link attached at right angles to it at the required distance above. The simplest method of attaching the hook length is to a loop in the line. But, especially when using live-bait, some freedom for the hook link is necessary. This can be secured by having swivels above and below the hook length or by using a three-way swivel with an attachment for the hook link in the middle.

The distance the bait on a paternoster will be above the bottom depends on the angle at which the line between rod and weight cuts the horizontal. If the paternoster is cast some distance so that the angle is comparatively narrow, allowance must be made and the hook line fixed much further from the weight to get the same distance from the bottom as if the paternoster were being fished under the rod point. You can use a float with the paternoster if it is adjusted to the exact depth of the water.

You detect bites by holding the line over a finger, any

interference with the taut line immediately making itself
felt. From the nature of the tackle, any fish taking a bait on
a paternoster will feel some resistance immediately. This
may not be so important with live-bait, but generally I think
it is a technique to be used only when there is none other
that will meet the case—fishing small holes. A paternoster
can have two or more hook lengths at suitable distances
above each other, but in fresh water this is rarely advisable.

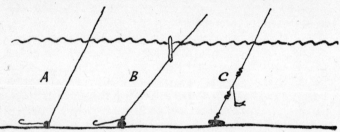

Fig. 10. Three ways of fishing. A: Normal ledger with pierced bullet.
B: Float ledger with line through ring of pear-shaped lead.
C: Paternoster

The one use of a two-hook paternoster, perhaps, would be
in searching for perch, when you might try a lobworm on the
bottom hook and a minnow on the upper one.

To make the simplest form of ledger, you thread your
line through a pierced weight, pinch on a shot below it so
that the weight cannot slide down and then attach your hook
anything from six to eighteen inches below. When this is
cast out, lead and bait lie on the bottom. If a fish takes the
bait, the line is quite free to move through the lead as it is
pulled. On the bank this bite is detected either by the line
being drawn off or the point of the rod being pulled down.

Ledgering is probably the method by which the greatest
number of large coarse fish are taken. Its advantage is that
although any weight necessary for long casting can be used,
this weight is not felt by the fish when it mouths the bait
and its suspicions are not aroused. In theory the only resis-

tance should be a little friction between line and lead as it slips through the hole. In practice there are some difficulties. The line between bait, lead and rod is probably rarely absolutely straight, although if the lead is drawn in a foot or two after casting there is a chance of the line being straightened on an unobstructed bottom. Then again, if the hole in the lead is made large to give easy passage to the cast, it is apt to get clogged with mud or other matter so that friction is increased.

To avoid this, the pierced bullets and coffin-shaped leads used for many years are giving way to pear-shaped weights in which the line passes through a small link swivel mounted in the lead, being stopped in the usual way with a shot.

In the past the rule has generally been a pierced bullet for still or sluggish water and a coffin-shaped lead for stronger currents. With the line passing through a swivel eye instead of the whole lead, a pear-shaped weight offers the advantage that the line will be held above the mud at the bottom.

As far as the size of the ledger is concerned, I think the smallest weight that can be cast and will hold the bottom should be the rule. Other considerations apart, when you hook a fish, it will have to lift the ledger-weight and if this is considerable the fish can put up no fight. In many cases a quarter-ounce weight will meet the case. The best distance between bait and weight, determined by the point at which you pinch your stopping shot, is much argued. In favour of a minimum distance, say six inches, is the argument that avoids the possibility of a fish being able to pick up and move the bait without drawing through line and registering a bite. When fishing with crust it is often a good plan to have the stop shot touching the hook eye so that when the ledger-lead lies on the bottom, the crust rests on top of it, hiding the lead from the fish and keeping the crust right on the bed of the river or lake.

Most anglers allow at least twelve inches and more

generally eighteen inches. This almost certainly means that many bites are not suspected at all. On the other hand it may encourage the fish to take the bait confidently.

Many anglers seem to regard ledgering as a pleasantly lazy way of fishing in which the rod can be put in a rest and there is nothing to do until the movement of its tip or of the line indicates a bite. Many make a habit of putting out a ledger with a second rod while they are swimming the stream with the other. But serious ledgering really requires holding the rod so that the most delicate bites can be detected and acted on immediately if they are of the right type—a slow pull. Short 'knocks' in contrast to the slow pull usually mean either very small fish or a fish that has not made up its mind yet.

If you put the rod in a rest, there are various ways of detecting a bite. A small piece of paste squeezed on the line immediately above the reel will make it sag. Any movement of the lump of paste indicates a fish is touching the bait. Another method is to bend a small piece of paper over the line, let it rest on the ground and put a small stone on it. Any pull on the line will result in the paper moving and catching your attention. For ledgering at night, now popular with anglers in search of specimen fish of some species, there are ingenious electrical bite-detectors. Any handyman can make one for himself, the essential being a very light switch round which the line is given a turn so that the slightest movement results in a buzzer sounding.

An alternative is the float ledger. The float is fixed at a distance from the ledger-weight which is determined by the depth of the water and the speed of the current and it is cocked by shot in the normal way, pinched on well above the ledger-weight. The ledger-weight and bait rest on the bottom. When the bait is taken and the line pulled through the ledger-weight, the float goes under.

There is another technique for holding the bait in one place which is called laying-on. It can be used in moderate

8. Fly-fishing for trout on a Welsh river. Here the side cast is essential to avoid the trees which almost meet overhead

9. A contrast to the Welsh river is the Hampshire Meon, a small river which holds many trout. Concealment is vital. The angler has just completed his upstream cast. Izaak Walton fished here

currents only. Slide the float up until it gives a depth which will allow one or two shot about nine inches from the hook to rest on the bottom. Cast out and instead of allowing the float to glide downstream as in swimming the stream, hold it stationary. When swimming the stream is producing no results, a change to laying-on, which keeps the bait still well on the bottom, often improves matters.

One or other of these techniques will enable you to get your bait to fish in almost every situation. But do not be hidebound by them. The most perfectly presented bait is wasted if it does not meet a fish, and a twenty-yard cast has no merit in itself and is a waste of time if the fish are feeding a yard from the bank under your rod tip. A bait tripping nicely along the bottom serves no purpose if the fish are feeding a foot under the surface. To meet situations where none of the orthodox methods with float or ledger will bring your bait and the fish together, you must be prepared to adapt and improvise. The surface-cruising carp will take no notice of a bait on the bottom and be alarmed by one held by a float six inches above it. A floating piece of bread might be the solution, but if it is cast near the carp it will disturb it and if it is cast much in advance, may break up before the carp reaches it.

The carp fisherman meets the situation by casting a piece of bread onto a lily pad where it can rest until the carp is near when he twitches it gently into the water. Or again, the big perch or chub may be in a hole under trees or bushes growing thickly over the water. You cannot cast into the place and there is no convenient current to carry your float down to it. You may decide reluctantly that the place is un-fishable and pass on. Or you can discard your float, put on sufficient weights a foot or eighteen inches from the hook to pull line through the rod rings, creep quietly up to the trees, push your rod cautiously through them horizontally until its tip is well over the water, and then release line so that the bait drops slowly down to the waiting fish . . .

How you will bring your fish to the bank when you have hooked it is another matter. Here is a case where you may be forced to use strong tackle. But generally the rule should be to fish as fine as possible, taking into account the size of fish you encounter and the force you may have to use to keep them away from snags and weeds. Although you sometimes hear anglers talking of being broken as if it were something to be proud of, there is no merit in it.

The way in which different fish behave when hooked varies, and I shall have some remarks on their individual characteristics in the next chapter. But in the case of good fish, the weakest part of the tackle will never be strong enough to enable the fish to be brought to the bank right away by main force. It must be played until it is sufficiently tired to be brought to the net under control. Actual experience of playing two or three good fish teaches more than a thousand words, but there are a few principles which should guide you.

To keep the fish under control, your line must always be taut. You can ensure this only if you keep your rod point well up. Your rod will bend as strain is exerted and if the fish changes direction or plunges suddenly, the springiness of the rod will even out the strain on the line and smooth out jerks which otherwise might break it.

If the fish draws off line, the check on your reel, plus the pressure of your finger or thumb on the spool, and the spring of your rod will brake sufficiently to tire him. Unless it is apparent he is going for a weed-bank or obstruction which will entangle your line, let him run. If a fish carries your line into weed, you may eventually get it free, but in the meantime the fish will probably have wriggled off the hook. In these circumstances you must either hold the fish hard and risk a break or try to make him stop or change his direction. The length of the rod can be used to guide the fish to a certain extent by exerting sidestrain. Even a determined fish will not travel very far when strain is being applied sideways. A fish dashes off when hooked because it resents its freedom of movement being restricted. A sudden relaxation of the restriction resulting from the rod being momentarily dipped sometimes stops a fish in its dash to a particular point.

If a fish turns and swims towards you, you must recover line as fast as possible to remain in contact and control. If your reel does not enable you to do this fast enough, do not hesitate (when fly-fishing) to take in the loose line with your left hand, taking care not to get the loops entangled in your feet. This loose line can be reeled in if there is a pause or paid out by hand if the fish dashes off again.

The behaviour of many anglers suggests that once a fish is hooked, they think concealment is no longer necessary. But a fish that is frightened will often find renewed strength as it comes to the bank and make a sudden dash. Do not dance about when playing a fish, and when you have coaxed it to the bank, get the net under it with as little movement and fuss as possible. The moment of netting may be the most dangerous of all. If the rim of the net hits the line, it is quite likely to break a light hook-hold and you will have the mortification of seeing your fish glide away at the moment of victory. The correct method is to have the net well submerged with its opening as nearly horizontal as possible. Draw the fish over the net rather than try to thrust the net under the fish and pull the net towards you before lifting it. Do not let the line become loose until the fish is at the bottom of the net, preferably head first. If you are wise you will never let an inexperienced companion or spectator help you by netting the fish. The odds are the fish will get a bang on the nose from the rim of the net and either the hook will tear loose or the line will break.

5

Coarse Fish and Baits

THE time has come to deal individually with the commoner kinds of coarse fish and the best techniques and baits to take them. By far the most widely pursued is the roach because it is so well distributed that it is likely to be found in every type of water, still and flowing. Once it has reached maturity it is a very shy feeder and thus a challenge to the angler's skill, calling for the finest tackle. Any roach over two pounds is noteworthy, and landing it on the fragile tackle generally required to deceive it is an achievement.

Whatever technique you use, fine tackle and immediate response to the slightest touch should be the rule. The roach takes a wide variety of baits. In order of preference they are gentles, paste and crust, but small red worms, wheat and, where it is permitted, hemp are also effective. Ground-baiting is essential, 'cloud' where the water is still, the bread and bran type, or the loose-fed maggots, where it is moving. If we must generalize about the best baits, probably the animal ones will be found most attractive in summer and the cereal ones in winter.

The roach is not built to swim strongly and you will not therefore find it in rivers where the current is heaviest. In summer seek them near weed-beds where the water is moving but not strong. In winter, when most of the heavier fish are caught, you will generally find them in deep water with a minimum of movement, but my experience is that, especially when the water is coloured, they may still be found in comparatively shallow water even in cold weather. In still water the roach may be almost anywhere and it is a question of picking a likely spot and seeking to collect the fish by ground-baiting. If this brings no results in an hour, the probability is there are no roach near and you should try another spot.

Roach feed near the bottom and on it, and at intermediate depths to the actual surface, but generally speaking a bait between half the water depth and the bottom is most killing. In still water, ledgering or float-fishing with a bait falling naturally through the water is good technique. In fast rivers, or in any fast part of a river, trotting or swimming down works well. In summer small baits do best, but in winter a good big-roach bait is a lobworm's tail. Fly-fishing for roach in summer and early autumn also pays off.

The silvery dace does not grow to the size of the roach. A half-pound dace is a good one in most waters, a pound dace is notable anywhere and the record is one pound four ounces four drams, from the Little Ouse at Thetford, Norfolk. But, as its slimmer shape suggests, the dace is livelier and, weight for weight, twice the fighter. Not many anglers go fishing specially for dace, unless it is with a fly, but in waters where they thrive, they can give excellent sport. Winter or summer dace are likely to be in faster water than roach and they are not often found in still water. Because they can move faster than roach, their natural diet contains a higher proportion of 'meat'. For this reason gentles and small red worms are the best baits with paste, bread and cereals a poor third. They are fast biters, but not particularly shy ones. A dace may sometimes be taken ledgering, but generally swimming the stream or long trotting with the bait just off the bottom is the best method. Ground-bait is essential to keep a shoal feeding in the swim and loose-feeding with maggots will often keep the shoal feeding well all day.

Rudd closely resemble roach in appearance, but their distribution is much more limited and they are fish of lakes and ponds rather than rivers. The simplest way of telling a rudd from a roach in case of doubt is to look at the mouth. The rudd's lower lip projects beyond the upper lip. The roach's upper lip projects beyond the lower. This formation suggests the rudd is a surface feeder and, in fact, it gives the best sport of all coarse fish on artificial fly. It will take gentles, small red worms and bread crust and generally the problem in bait-fishing is how to present the bait high up in the water without disturbing the fish. Because they are surface feeders, ground-baiting in the usual way is not much use. The method is to tie half a slice of bread to a small stone with a piece of string or nylon a little longer than the depth of the water. When this is thrown in, the bread floats and if there are rudd about they will soon be seen attacking it. This method of ground-baiting can be used when fly-fishing for rudd, with perhaps a single gentle on a size 14 or 16 hook substituted for an artificial fly, by far the most interesting as well as effective way of catching rudd.

With the chub we come to an altogether heavier fish. The average weight varies a good deal. On some waters, a three-pound chub is something to talk about. On others, double this weight would be a good fish, but not a record. For size, the best chub water is probably the Hampshire Avon, where fish over seven pounds have been taken. When it is hooked the chub makes a very powerful dash with all its weight behind it seeking some underwater tree roots or some other bolthole. It is true that if it does not succeed with its first dash a chub gives up much more quickly than a trout half its size, but his power calls for stronger tackle than the fish we have been dealing with. At the same time the chub is shy, not so much in taking the bait like a roach as about any disturbance or movement.

You will generally find chub in smooth, gently flowing water, behind a pile, in a backwater under trees, anywhere it is not called on to battle with the current but can rely on food being brought down or dropping from bushes and trees above. To compensate for his shyness, he has an indiscriminate appetite and it is not easy to think of anything edible which, at some time, may not take a chub. Lobworms, a bunch of gentles, paste (preferably with cheese) are favourites, but when available, wasp grubs, caterpillars, slugs and even small frogs are taken. The chub is not averse to a small live-bait if it comes within reach. If it can be presented to him without arousing suspicion, he will grab a large, fuzzy artificial fly, undoubtedly mistaking it for a caterpillar which has dropped from a tree.

The chub can be taken by swimming the stream, long trotting or ledgering. The method chosen is likely to be decided by the nature of the water to be fished. The technique is the same as that for roach, with the difference that the chub does not go about in large shoals and that therefore ground-baiting should be moderate and even limited to throwing in from time to time small fragments of something of the same type as your hook-bait. If you are after chub, you must be prepared to move on when you have taken one or two fish from a swim or if you fail to get any response in half an hour.

For the angler who measures his sport by the total weight of a day's catch, there can be no freshwater fish to equal bream. In the right place and in the right conditions, catches of bream have exceeded a hundredweight, thirty, forty and more fish of three pounds and upwards each. But this does not mean the bream is the duffer's delight. You have first to find your bream. The shape of the fish, often likened to a plate, indicates it is not able to deal with strong currents. Bream waters are lakes, canals and sluggish rivers. Many bream waters are almost featureless and sport depends on locating a shoal. Bream are great wanderers in search of food. Sometimes they give away their presence by rolling on the surface, but generally unless you can get advice from an experienced local angler you will have to pick a likely spot where the water is deep and slow and rely on ground-baiting.

Ideally several pounds of bread and bran mixture should

71

be thrown into your chosen swim the night before. You can afford to be generous with ground-bait for bream. Shoals are generally large and the fish can dispose of many pounds of food without their appetite being satisfied. The big catches are made by judicious ground-baiting to keep the shoal round while the fish are taken one by one.

Gentles, paste and worms are the favoured baits. Both ledger and fishing well on the bottom with a float are good, but bream also feed at mid-water at times. Many bream specialists start with a ledger and, when the presence of a shoal is indicated by a bite, change over to float tackle.

Bream stop feeding when the water temperature drops below the middle forties so that fishing for them is largely restricted to the period from the opening of the season to mid-October. An hour before sunrise and two hours after sunrise are undoubtedly the best, and although bream may be taken at any time, especially in September and early October, the angler who chooses his hours of fishing to suit his normal sleeping habits is never likely to make a great catch.

When hooked the bream does not run but bores downwards. Playing this fish rarely presents difficulties unless it gets into heavy water outside the swim so that the strain of the current is added to the bream's weight. Even where the bream run to five or six pounds, a line of two to three pounds b.s. is sufficient and match fishermen take them on much finer tackle.

With tench also it is the early worm that succeeds. This need be no hardship, and if June 16th dawns fine, there is no better way to welcome the new season than at a lakeside watching your float in the first light. Although tench are found in some sluggish rivers, they are essentially fish of muddy lakes with plenty of weed and lilies. The most likely place is beside one of these patches. Your tackle must be strong, say six pounds b.s., to keep a hooked fish away from the weeds and give a reasonable chance of dealing with it should it get in. At the same time, the tench is a suspicious fish and from this point of view, the finer the better.

I find a worm unquestionably the best bait, but there are some waters where paste and maggots give better results. Using all the knowledge and skill possible, you still need luck to catch a good tench. Raking a swim in the weeds with a rake on a rope the night before fishing stirs up the bottom-living insects and attracts shoals of tench. Groundbaiting the night before with bread, meal and maggots and worms also helps, as with bream fishing. In the absence of wind, my choice would be fishing on the bottom with the lightest possible float. The first indication that a tench is after the bait is often very tentative. Striking at this is likely to be unproductive. The float will often quiver and gyrate for long minutes before moving off and slowly submerging, or it may lie flat on the surface. Then is the time to tighten into your fish. Tench fight deep and very hard so you must be both firm yet delicate in your handling of them.

Tench feed best when the temperature is over 60 and under 70 degrees. Fishing for it virtually ends in October. In general it becomes progressively more difficult to catch tench as the season advances. Ideal conditions for catching tench are likely if there is a spell of fine, settled weather at the end of June and beginning of July.

If the king of coarse fish had to be named from the point of view of fighting, probably most anglers would vote for the barbel. There are fish which run to greater weights, but unlike many coarse fish, the barbel not only makes a first dash of great power, but also keeps up the struggle until it is beaten. Unfortunately, barbel are not widely distributed or found in great numbers and appear to be becoming scarcer, perhaps because of pollution. Deliberately fishing for barbel, except in certain definite river reaches where they are known to thrive, mostly on the Thames and Hampshire Avon, Kennet, Swale, Wharfe, Dorset Stour and Severn, is a chancy business. Anglers after other fish who hook a barbel by chance are likely to be broken by the surprising power of its first rush which follows a feeling that the hook has got snagged on the bottom. If you go out definitely after barbel, you will have to be prepared for blank days, but once you have caught a good barbel, you will probably think they are worth it.

The barbel is a fish of fast clean water, running over gravel. The Avon-type rod and line of four to seven pounds breaking strain, depending on the average size of fish for the river, will be suitable, but be prepared for prolonged battles. The practical method in most barbel swims is the ledger. It was formerly the custom to ground-bait barbel swims well before with hundreds and even thousands of worms. Nowadays the worms are not available and bread and bran is used. But the worm is a good bait and, if it is used, a few should be thrown in with the ground-bait. Gentles, cheese and luncheon meat are the alternative baits and the evidence suggests they are little if any less successful than worms provided the barbel are there.

No fish has received more attention in the last decade from serious anglers than the carp. Twenty years ago there were many anglers who had caught carp up to five and even ten pounds and very many more, like myself, with memories while roach-fishing in some lake of suddenly finding themselves into a fish apparently making for the horizon leaving them with a thumping heart and broken line. The general opinion was that really big carp—the existence of fish of twenty pounds and up was proved—were uncatchable because by the time the carp grew large it was so wary that it was impossible to present a bait it would accept on tackle strong enough to hold it.

Now there are carp in more waters due to constant stocking from Italian and Dutch sources, and more anglers now know how to catch them and have the necessary tackle with which to do it. Richard Walker's record forty-four pounder lived for years in the London Zoo aquarium—a challenge to many carp addicts.

The carp lives in still waters, generally lakes with plentiful weed growth to increase the problem of the angler both in casting and playing. In high summer, high day temperatures and the great caution of the big carp makes night or very late or early fishing essential. The carp takes a bait cautiously, but likes one in keeping with its size. It has a big mouth and the angler has to think of baits on quite a different scale from those he generally uses. There is probably no bait a big carp will not take—large ones have been taken on a spoon. But chiefly because they will not be troubled by fish of other species, the specialist carp-fishers restrict themselves either to a piece of crust two inches long or a potato the size of a golf ball or cubes of canned meat. But there are also exotic baits called 'specials', concocted from high protein materials, or with plenty of smell (as well) which are used to lure carp. Some are also proof against any fish but carp!

Technique and equipment have become extremely specialized, but the ordinary angler is likely to compromise, at least at first. You could use your spinning-rod with line of ten pounds b.s., but in reasonably open water the Avon rod and six- to seven-pound line will cope with fish up to twenty pounds. Bait presentation is important. The slightest resistance is liable to result in the bait being hastily dropped or ignored. The carp fisherman therefore aims to present it either on a ledger in which the line can be drawn off with an absolute minimum of resistance, the rod pointing directly at the bait to reduce friction, or, when it is possible to have no weight at all, the hook being tied directly on the line. Ground-baiting should be generous and, preferably, carried out up to three days before fishing, especially if the carp have to be 'educated' to a new bait like potato.

It is impossible even to summarize the exact techniques in a few lines. But in a nutshell they consist of casting into the

chosen swim and leaving the rod in rests so that the line—
yards of it if necessary—can be drawn off without the
slightest check. There follows a period of waiting, which
may be measured in hours rather than minutes during
which the greatest caution must be observed, before the
line is seen to be going away. It may be slowly, when great
patience is called for, or it may be fast and steadily, in
which case there is an immediate strike. If the carp is
hooked, it will make a run that may not be checked for
fifty yards. Whether the battle ends in a few minutes with a
broken line or a hook pulled out or in half an hour with a
twenty-pound carp wallowing exhausted near the bank
depends on the angler.

Floating crust is also a killing method. This may be cast
gently to fish seen moving on top among weeds, and quite
often the fish will suck down the crust quickly.

It is only right to say from experience that, as with
salmon, this is a form of angling where you could work
hard for a week and never touch a fish. But the consistent
success of the specialist shows it is not a matter of luck.
Anglers may argue about whether a big carp or a big barbel
provides the greatest thrill of coarse fishing, but perhaps the
verdict must go to the carp because it may be so much
bigger and because the tenseness of the waiting, often in
darkness, adds to the sense of drama.

Except for the gudgeon, bleak and other fish whose
weight rarely exceeds a couple of ounces and which interest
the angler only as live-bait or makeweight in matchfishing,
the other common coarse fish are predators. Vegetarian
baits are of no interest to them and ground-baiting of little
or no use, although the fine particles may attract small fish
which in turn attract the predators. The boldest of them is
the perch, especially when young, and it is generally the
easiest of all freshwater fish to catch. When it has grown to
a couple of pounds or more, the perch is just as voracious,
but quickly alarmed and therefore not easy to catch.

Perch, easily identified by their spiny dorsal fins, black stripes and red fins, were widely distributed in lakes, canals and all but the fastest rivers but in the late sixties, early seventies were reduced by disease. If you catch one without unduly alarming the others, you are likely to take others at regular intervals until the shoal moves off. As with most shoals, the fish are more or less the same size and the larger the fish, the fewer in a shoal. If you catch a half-pounder, you may get many more, but if you catch one of two pounds or more, you probably will not get another as the shoal would be of only three or four which made off alarmed by the fight. In fishing for large perch, therefore, it pays to move from place to place, seeking out the fish rather than trying to gather them to you.

The most likely spots in summer are near weed-beds. If you approach cautiously you can often see the fish in shallow water. In autumn perch go into deeper water. At all times they avoid water moving rapidly, conserving their energy for a dash after prey. They feed throughout the season, but come into condition rather late so that fishing is generally at its best from September onwards.

For big perch, especially in late summer and autumn, the best bait is a minnow which can be fished either well off the bottom with float tackle or with a paternoster which makes it possible to search small openings in weed-beds, holes and backwaters and other restricted places. If nothing happens in ten minutes, move on to try another place. A large worm is the alternative, fished either with float or ledger. In the latter case it pays to keep the worm moving by pulling in a foot of line at short intervals. This method can almost amount to spinning the bait along the bottom very slowly. Like all predatory fish, perch can be taken on a spinner, spoon, or plug and this is the most interesting way of angling for them once the weeds have died down.

The perch does not run when hooked, turning to a new direction as soon as it feels restraint. But it does not give up easily and as the hookhold is generally delicate, you must play the fish with caution and not try to force it into the net.

The pike is the tyrant amongst freshwater fish. The only thing he has to fear is a larger pike and all other fish are his prey. You will find him in almost every piece of water where he has not been deliberately exterminated as vermin, even in quite fast rivers where his shape and strength enable him to overcome the current. But normally he does not waste energy chasing his prey. His method is to remain motionless, suspended in the water, relying on his stillness and camouflage to bring a small fish within a foot or two. Then the pike moves too fast for the eye to follow. The prey is seized across the middle in the fearsome teeth from which there is no escape. The pike may make his meal on the spot, but more often cruises gently off before turning the smaller fish so that it can be swallowed head first. The pike's vision is more binocular than that of most fish and he can see objects above and around in a wide area. But except in that last dash, the pike is a lazy fish, and the bait has to be brought within a few feet or it will generally be ignored.

To my mind there is only one enjoyable and sporting way of catching pike and that is spinning. But this is impossible in many waters during summer and autumn because of weed. The only alternative is bait-fishing with another fish. alive or dead. Live-baiting can be carried out either with paternoster or float, the float having the advantage that it is easy to alter the depth at which the bait is fished. Fishing with a dead-bait on a ledger or on wobbling or spinning mount, is also killing. It is not even necessary to use a freshwater fish. A small herring or sprat from the fishmonger will serve and it is worth trying the sink and draw method suggested for perch.

Whatever the method, the trace next to the hooks must be of wire to give protection against the pike's teeth which will easily sever nylon. That does not mean using a miniature hawser. Pike may be bold, but they are not foolish. A single strand of the six to fourteen pounds b.s. special wire now made will be almost as invisible as nylon.

In summer you will find pike in backwaters, in quiet spots alongside weed-beds and near the mouths of ditches and tributaries. In winter, it goes into deeper water and it is essential to get the bait well down. The pike's habit of seizing its prey and taking it off means that unless you are using snap-tackle you must not strike immediately but give it line and time to get the hooks inside the mouth. A hard strike is needed to drive the hooks home in the tough mouth. Playing a pike is not usually a very exciting experience unless, as sometimes happens, you have hooked it accidentally on roach tackle when pulling in a small fish. A pike generally makes a vigorous first rush, shaking its head to free itself, but soon gives up, and a big pike can be disappointing, 'coming in like a log'.

The number of anglers who deliberately fish for eels must be small, and they are probably more concerned with a tasty supper than with sport. To most anglers eels are just a nuisance which can make fishing with anything but paste impossible on occasions. But there is quite a thrill from catching a big eel deliberately. Eels will take gentles or a worm, but unquestionably the best bait for big ones is a dead fish. Any kind of fish up to four inches in length will do. Eels scavenge on the bottom and a ledger is the best tackle. You need a wire trace because of the eel's sharp teeth and a ten pound b.s. line because playing an eel in the ordinary sense is impossible and attempting it is likely simply to result in an appalling tangle.

As soon as your eel is hooked, hold firm and bring it straight in. But do not be in a hurry to strike. Let the eel draw off all the line it wants. The normal thing is for this drawing off to be followed by a pause and it is on the next movement that you strike. Having got your eel onto the bank—using a landing-net only complicates things—an undignified struggle will probably follow. I have found no easy way to avoid it. In theory an eel subsides under a powerful blow on the back above the vent, but those who give this advice do not tell how to aim your blow at a wriggling eel. You have to deal with your eel as best you can, perhaps cutting the line and dropping it into a sack.

Grayling are classed as coarse fish because their spawning season coincides with that of roach, perch and the rest rather than with the trout which they more closely resemble in habits. They need clean, fast water and, except that they come into condition in September just as trout-fishing is finishing, they are caught by the same methods as trout. Since they take the artificial fly freely, fly-fishermen welcome them as providing sport during the close season for trout. But for the angler who wants to stick to bait, they offer the opportunity of dealing with a game fish.

Gentles in autumn and a small worm in winter are the usual baits. Because of the water they invariably inhabit—strong glides in clear rivers—swimming the stream or long trotting are really the only methods possible. Grayling are not shy biters, and if you miss a bite, the grayling will probably come again unless it has been alarmed by seeing you. Because the water is usually rough as it passes over a stony bottom, the best float is a little sphere. Aim to have the bait two or three inches from the bottom so that it searches all the likely places and the slightest check should result in an immediate strike. The grayling is a game fighter, fully the equal of most trout of the same size. It seems to favour dashing downstream, taking advantage of the current. The answer must be, if the bank allows it, always to try to get below the fish.

10. Spinning in the River Tay. Scotland has thousands of miles of fishing in magnificent scenery

11. Fishing for bass from the beach at Porthcurno, Cornwall. Bass are often to be found only a few yards behind the breaking waves which stir up and wash down food

12. The end of the battle. A salmon is brought to the net. This photograph was taken on the River Laerdal in Norway

13. Weight for age! Thirteen-year-old Tore Sandberg landed a fish most anglers only dream about—a thirteen-pound trout

6

Learning to Spin

CASTING a dead fish or artificial lure and then retrieving it so that its movement makes it appear alive is one of the most effective and interesting ways of catching all the predatory fish—perch, pike, trout, sea-trout and salmon. Recent experiences and experiments have shown that any coarse fish, especially early in the season when fry are plentiful, may take a spinning bait, but normally it is only an effective lure for the species which habitually prey on smaller fish.

Until the invention of the fixed-spool reel, the mere mechanics of casting a lure for spinning required considerable skill and practice. Using a centre-pin reel requires for nice judgement in braking with a finger or thumb so that the drum does not overrun when the bait strikes the water and produce a bird's nest of tangled line. The difficulty is reduced with a multiplier if it has some device for automatically adjusting the speed of the revolutions to the pull of the line. But it was the fixed-spool reel which changed everything and made it possible for anyone to master the simple mechanics of casting with reasonable accuracy in an hour. Those who mastered casting with a centre pin may prefer to stick to it, but nine out of ten anglers in the future will prefer the fixed spool. A common criticism now is that the fixed-spool reel has made spinning altogether too easy and mechanical to be sporting. But this implies there is nothing to spinning except casting a lure and reeling it up again. There is much more to it.

The mastery of the mechanics of casting, with whatever kind of reel, is only the foundation of success in spinning.

F   81

The choice of lure, and where and how to work it in the water for different fish under different conditions, will, even more than skill in casting, decide the number of fish that are taken. An indifferent caster with an 'eye for water' and a knowledge of the habits of fish who concentrates on the behaviour of his lure under the water will generally take more fish and bigger ones than the angler who is satisfied simply to make long casts and reel in. Ability to cast a long distance is useful, of course, but in practice probably as many fish are taken five yards from the rod as thirty yards from it.

The general rules of concealment and quiet apply as much to spinning as to any other method of angling. The depth at which a lure moves is as important as its speed and direction. This is decided by a combination of factors. The heavier the lure (and the weights on the line), the deeper it will normally swim at a given speed. The faster the retrieve, the higher the lure will swim, except with plug baits. Where the speed of the current is appreciable, it will affect the minimum speed you must retrieve to give movement to the lure. If you are drawing it downstream, you must retrieve more quickly to get a spin. If you are drawing the lure against the current, a slower rate of retrieve will produce movement and, in a fast stream, you might get it while simply holding the lure stationary. The height of your rod point and the angle at which you hold it will also affect the depth. Only experience can teach how to combine these factors so that the lure moves at the speed and depth you have decided are the most effective in the conditions. This should be no more a matter of chance than the decision at what depth to fish under a float.

The most helpful way of dealing with a big subject may be to describe the different types of lure and the ways in which they can be used under different conditions for various fish. Spinning baits are either natural or artificial, but even natural ones must be given artificial movement to make them seem alive. The common natural baits are minnows, sprats and small roach or dace. The general experience is that in most conditions a natural spinning bait is more deadly than a wholly artificial one of metal, plastic, wood and other materials. A spinning bait has to be taken fairly quickly—there is not much scope for a fish to nose around it as it might a lump of paste. The advantage of the natural bait therefore probably arises from the sense of smell. Other things being equal, a real fish may less often result in last-minute doubts being aroused. If this is the case, there is an advantage in having fresh rather than preserved baits.

To make the dead fish attractive in the water, special tackle is necessary. A spinning flight consists of a pair of metal or plastic fins fixed at the head of a fine steel wire which may be partly encased in lead to increase weight. Two or more triple

FIG. 11. Archer-type tackle for spinning natural bait

hooks lie behind the fins. The steel is pushed into the mouth of the fish until the fins fit closely to its head and it is further secured by one hook of each triangle into the flesh. A swivel at the head and others in the trace enable the fish to turn freely in the water and prevent the line being twisted.

In practice friction at the swivels always results in some turns being imparted to the line and preventing kinking is one of the spinner's major concerns. A bait will spin clockwise or anti-clockwise according to the angle of the fins. Using in turn baits which spin in opposite directions helps to keep the line kink-free. Alternatively, or additionally, you can use an anti-kink lead in which any tendency of the swivels not to turn is countered by the weight. Actually, for the peace of mind they give, it is better to buy ball-bearing swivels, as they prevent kinking.

Instead of being made to turn, the dead-bait can be made to wobble. The flight for this is the same but without fins, the wobble being produced by curving the fish slightly between the hook triangles. Instead of travelling straight when pulled, the fish will wobble. Part of the effect is greatly to increase its apparent size.

Artificial lures are made in countless patterns and in sizes from half an inch to six inches or more in length. They fall into broad classes, each with its characteristic move-ments and uses. Devons are torpedo-shaped pieces of silver or gold metal or wood or plastic with fins to make them spin and a triangle of hooks at the tail. A metal Devon sinks quickly when it strikes the water and must be kept moving fairly fast to make it spin. The second class is made up of the spoons which, basically, are exactly what they sound

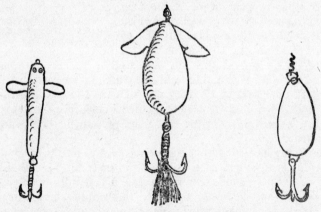

Three spinning lures: Fig. 12. Devon. Fig. 13. Colorado spoon. Fig. 14. Standard spoon

like, handleless metal spoons in silver or other colours with a triangle of hooks behind them. When pulled through the water, they wobble and dart and may be considered the artificial equivalent of the natural bait arranged to wobble.

Spoons are made in an immense variety of shapes and types, with new ones appearing every year. In some, the spoon is free to move round a shaft—bar-spoons. The shape may be that of a kidney or other asymmetrical form. The spoon may be accompanied by tufts of red wool when it is known as a Colorado. Each pattern has its characteristic appearance and action in the water. Every angler usually finds one or two favourites, and probably on many occasions the way the spoon is worked in the water is of more importance than particular variations in pattern.

The third class are the plugs, introduced from America and, after some scepticism, becoming increasingly popular with British anglers. Plugs do not, in fact, spin, and this is an advantage as it diminishes the dangers of kinking the line. The plug, usually with triangles at head and tail hanging underneath, is shaped from wood or plastic, and may be lighter or heavier than water. If it is a floater, it is shaped to dive and wobble when drawn through the water. In weedy or snaggy water a halt brings the plugs to the surface, to be drawn over the snag. Sinkers also have a side-to-side wobble.

The success of plugs has led to their being produced in an astonishing variety of shapes and colours with names as strange and imaginative as their appearance. Many anglers find them irresistible. If you are buying a selection, consider their atttraction for fish and not for yourself. Don't take your wife with you or you will end up with a collection of 'pets'!

Each of these classes of lures requires to be worked in a different way, and which you use must depend on your quarry and the conditions. Let us take the species one by one. Roach and the other normally 'vegetarian' coarse fish are generally taken more effectively by other methods. If you want to spin for them, bear in mind that their mouths are not constructed like those of the predatory fish, so that the artificial must be small, perhaps a spoon of the type usually called a fly-spoon, no more than half an inch long and fitted with a single hook. Fish it slowly near the bottom. The most likely spots would be near the banks where these fish might expect to encounter fry.

For perch, I have found the modern bar-spoons (half to one inch) the best of the artificials. A Devon would have to be spun too fast for effective use with any coarse fish.

The natural minnow is better fished on the sink and draw principle than spun. Artificial lures are apt to be armed with heavy hooks. You do not want these coarse ones for perch and they are liable to tear out. If necessary, slip the triangle out and fit a finer, if not a smaller, one with a split ring.

FIG. 15. Fly-spoon

You will not find perch in strong currents, and spinning should be as slow as possible consistent with keeping the lure lifelike. Weeds and other obstructions make spinning difficult or impossible in many of the most likely perch haunts. Here try a natural minnow on a weighted flight. Cast out and allow to sink to the bottom, then jerk it up to the surface. Let it sink and repeat until the cast is fished out.

Although a pike can swim fast for a short distance, it does not expect to have to work for a meal. It hunts by ambush rather than hot pursuit. A Devon can be moved at a speed slow enough for pike only when being spun upstream in a current that would be too fast to harbour a pike. The spinning baits for pike, in order of effectiveness in my experience, are natural fish, spoons and plugs. Any fish except perhaps a gudgeon, which does not flash well, will serve—and it does not have to be too small, although in comparing the size with a live-bait, remember that the spun or wobbled bait is apt to look larger in water through the phenomenon of persistence of vision. Big baits for big pike is a fairly sound rule, and if the water is known to contain a monster, you can try a herring.

Autumn and winter, when the weeds are down, is the time when spinning for them comes into its own. If weeds are still troublesome, a plug can be fished in places where a spoon or spinning bait would be hopelessly hung up. The particular fascination of the plug on or near the surface is that you often see the lure being pursued and taken.

Generally, the colder the water, the further down you must search. Probably the commonest reasons for pike being missed is the lure being moved too quickly and too high, and this may apply in summer as well as in deep water.

In many cases you will be faced with an apparently rather featureless piece of water. You know there are pike in it, but exactly where you can only speculate. Fish never take up a position altogether by accident, but the bottom features which decide where the pike is hunting are hidden and you have no alternative but a systematic search of the water. Start with a cast of half your maximum distance up the bank, either to your left or right, and work round with casts like the spokes of a wheel, yourself being the hub. Then repeat the casts at double the distance. In this way you avoid missing water or covering it twice.

Whatever lure you are using, fish it at constantly varying speeds, aiming at a series of darting, staggering movements rather than a steady run. In this way you cover the water in depth to a degree and, more important, your lure resembles an injured fish. It seems a natural instinct for wild things to kill their injured fellows, and in any case, the pike seems particularly attracted to an injured fish, perhaps because it promises an easy kill. Never reel in steadily when spinning for pike, although when using a well-made plug it is often most effective on a slow straight recovery.

Most pike lures are silver, golden or copper, or red in whole or part. Your choice must depend on your estimate of their visibility in the circumstances. The general rule is gold or copper for gloomy days or coloured water, silver for bright days and clear water. There are anglers who swear by a lure with some red in it for all conditions. I keep it in reserve, for use especially when a pike has come after a lure and then turned away at the last moment. The theory is that the pike, although not normally very suspicious, found something wrong and is more likely to come again to something different than to what he has already refused. But this refusal of a lure is often due, I think, to the angler consciously or unconsciously slowing it down when he sees it is pursued. Some writers, in fact, advocate this, although others advise speeding up to help the fish make up its mind! Better, I think, to keep the lure moving as before, as any new change of pace may raise doubts in that last second when it is about to be grabbed.

On some trout waters spinning is not permitted at all and on others allowed only in the later months of the season. Where it is permitted, it can be effective when a fly will produce no response. The fixed-spool reel which makes it possible to cast very light baits and get them moving the moment they hit the water allows spinning in shallows where a heavily weighted lure would almost certainly get hung up. The orthodox method of spinning for trout has been to cast across and reel in slowly as the current swings the lure towards your own bank. The current itself imparts sufficient movement to make the lure lifelike and it may be necessary to do no more than hold it until it has ceased to swing across the current. As it reaches the end of its swing, reel in, pulling it upstream.

But especially in mid-summer when rivers are low and clear, success is more likely with upstream spinning. The trout will be lying with their heads upstream so that you can stand in their blind area and, if you are wading, any disturbance of the water will only affect the parts downstream which you have already covered. As the lure is coming down downstream, it must be made to move fairly rapidly to avoid sinking and scraping along the bottom. For success you need small lures, the finest traces and lines and an eye for water. Before you cast, sweep your eye over the water you can reach, working out where the fish are likely to be and where you should cast so that your lure passes within easy reach. The tails of pools and deep water where the current changes direction at a bend are always promising. Trout take shelter behind stones to make quick forays into the strong water. Sometimes the movement of the surface water indicates the presence of a hiding place of this kind below. And don't neglect the water at the edges of the stream, even though it may be less than a foot deep. In a fast, rocky stream, a lure is apt to knock up against stones and you should examine the hooks at frequent intervals to make sure they have not been blunted or even had their points knocked off. It is infuriating to hook a good fish and then lose it almost immediately because the hook has been broken.

The first choice for trout amonst lures must be a natural minnow, made either to spin or wobble. It is not always easy to get a supply of fresh minnows, and in some streams almost impossible to spin the most likely spots without the minnows being badly knocked about so that the rate of replacement is high.

A small Devon artificial is hardly less effective, and I prefer one heavy enough to cast without additional weights to twist and get caught up. A one- to one-and-a-half-inch spoon with a single hook is good, but because of its lack of weight easier to present with a fly-rod. Small bar-spoons are also excellent. The same applies to a natural minnow fished by the sink and draw method, which can be particularly deadly when trout are lethargic in low water if you can get near enough to present it without alarming them. I cannot speak of the possibilities of small plugs from personal experience, but they might well prove effective on lakes, especially in the weedy shallows where it would be difficult to spin a Devon. A very small plug might also be effective for working over a rising fish which will often take a natural minnow spun just under the surface.

Spinning is a most effective way of taking sea-trout, especially if the water is slightly coloured, when a small silver Devon or bar-spoon may prove the best lure. A natural minnow on a spinning flight or a brown and green imitation are generally the best lures in clear water where success depends on concealment and finding the places where the fish are lying. This is rarely in deep water. In most rivers sea-trout will be found in the streams and glides from two to four feet deep. In daytime, at least, upstream spinning is essential. If you hook a fish, try to get it downstream as quickly as possible, as it will probably be one of a shoal from which you will be able to take several more if you can avoid alarming them. The commonest mistakes in spinning for sea-trout, I think, are spinning too-deep waters and using too-large lures. In most conditions a one-inch lure is quite big enough.

The average angler for coarse fish is apt to think of salmon-fishing as a difficult, esoteric and expensive sport. The plain fact is that if you can spin for pike, you can catch salmon and that your spinning-rod with 100 to 150 yards of eight to twelve pounds b.s. line will serve very well. As for being expensive, it is true that most of the favoured places command very high rents, but it is still possible to find salmon-fishing for around a pound a day. There will be many days when not a fish is seen or touched, perhaps, but the thrill of fighting a salmon makes these well worth enduring.

Consistent success in salmon-fishing depends on many things, not all of them in the control of the angler—water and weather conditions, the number of fish running up the river, local knowledge. Success is dependent on knowing where the salmon are lying, and this will vary with the state of the water. The beginner must rely on others with experience to give him advice on this. The places where salmon are likely to be lying having been found, the essentials are to spin deep and slowly. Cast from a spot where your line going out at an angle of about 45 degrees downstream will bring the lure slowly across the salmon's lie. Try and avoid letting the current produce a bulge in the line or the lure may be taken and ejected before you feel anything. When you feel a check, strike hard to drive the hooks home. If it is certain the fish is there, persistence pays. It is surprising how often a fish that has taken no notice will take on the third or fourth offering, and if all fails, it can be 'rested' while you fish another spot to return later.

The Devon probably remains the best all-round lure, the rule being a blue and silver one of two to three inches for coloured water and a brown and gold one of one and a half to two inches for clear water. A natural minnow can be substituted for the silver Devon and a sprat for the gold.

Although the 45 degree downstream cast is perhaps the easiest you can, of course, cast in any direction provided it will result in the lure being presented in the way you want —moving as slowly as possible, but naturally, broadside on to the salmon which will always be lying with its head facing upstream.

In summer, with low clear water, upstream casting with one-and-a-quarter Devons, quill minnows or bar-spoons, and retrieving faster than the current back downstream is very effective.

7

Fly-fishing

TO MOST people fly-fishing means fishing for trout, sea-trout or salmon. But many coarse fish can be caught on artificial flies and game fish can be taken by the methods commonly used for coarse fish. Fly-fishermen are sometimes apt to assume that theirs is a very special and superior form of angling. But from the purely technical viewpoint, the skill required to cast a float lightly and exactly thirty yards away is as great as that required to cast a fly the same distance. Learning to cast a fly is no harder than learning many other angling techniques.

It is true that, pound for pound, game fish fight harder than coarse fish. But this remains true whether they are caught on a worm or on an artificial fly. Fly-fishing has been plagued by a quite unnecessary snobbery and even mystery which discourages many from trying it. The all-round angler should master fly-fishing because, quite apart from the pleasure it will give him, in certain conditions it is the most effective and even the only way of taking fish. But it is also good exercise and the waters suitable for fly-fishing generally provide the pleasure of good scenery. Above all, perhaps, casting to a rising fish, no matter whether it is a trout or a chub, offers a special thrill and satisfaction, because you set out to deceive a particular fish in a particular way.

To attempt to deal with fly-fishing in all its aspects in a single chapter would be absurd, and here I can do no more than give sufficient information to encourage the novice or bottom-fisherman to forget the idea that fly-fishing is immensely difficult and try his hand. There is no end to learning in this branch of angling, but the essential knowledge required to make a start is not great.

Fly-fishing is commonly divided into two categories, according to whether the fly is fished on or under the surface. The dry fly, floating on the surface, is designed to imitate one or other of the many natural flies which hatch, alight or fall on to the water. The wet or sunken fly may sometimes be taken by fish for a drowned fly, but more often as a nymph —the fly before it has hatched—or one of the innumerable forms of water insect or even a minnow.

We use artificial flies tied with feathers, silk and other materials because the natural ones are generally useless as baits. They are too small or fragile to be impaled on a hook or to stand the strain of being cast. When natural flies are used in special conditions, they are not cast but dapped or allowed to be blown on to the water at the end of a fine silk line. Libraries have been written about the design and choice of artificial flies. If you become fascinated by fly-fishing, you will certainly turn to some of these books and learn a great deal. But the only effect on the novice is often hopeless confusion at the countless patterns and dressings. All you need to make a start and have the encouragement of catching fish can be given in a few paragraphs.

The first fly-fishermen used the bigger natural flies and naturally when the idea occurred of using an imitation that was more robust, the tendency was to try to make an exact reproduction of the natural fly. Confusion arose through failure to consider the likeness from the trout's viewpoint rather than the angler's. From what I have written about the vision of fish, it will be obvious that how a fish sees anything floating above or beside him in the water will be very different from how the angler sees the same object in air. Colour and shape may be changed and even size may be judged in a different way.

All flies are not made as exact reproductions of a natural

food of the fish. On dry land the artificial may bear no more resemblance to any natural fly than a spoon does to the small roach for which a pike mistakes it. Many wet flies are undoubtedly taken as minnows or fry. All the angler needs is an arrangement of feathers, tinsel, silk and so on which on or in the water will deceive a fish long enough —it may be for only a second—to encourage it to take it in its mouth. You have only to look at the scores of artificial mayflies, with and without wings and in all colours from palest yellow to nearly black, to appreciate this. None of them look in the least like the wonderful insects whose dancing and fluttering by the river makes the trout-angler's blood race in anticipation, but all of them will, on occasions, deceive a trout when cast on the water.

Many anglers collect a vast selection of flies, and then find nine-tenths of them are never used but that the supplies of half a dozen patterns need constant replenishment. There are even stories of anglers who fished right through a whole day or even a whole season with a single fly and caught as many or more fish as the next man who constantly changed his fly. They may be true. If they seem to make nonsense of the millions of words that have been written about choosing the right fly, it may be because the 'right' fly is always the one which a fish will take and its decision may be much more influenced by presentation than anything else. Next may come the size of the fly and last of all the colouring and pattern.

I am reluctant to suggest an ideal selection of half a dozen flies for trout, because this must vary with the type of water. But if you have March Brown, Wickham's Fancy and Greenwell's Glory in wet and dry patterns in two sizes, supplemented by two or three locally favoured flies, you will probably catch as many fish as the man with fly boxes carrying fifty different patterns.

For coarse fish, the selection of a fly is even simpler. The species mainly caught on fly are dace, chub, rudd, roach and perch, although pike, too, may be taken using flies between one and a half and two and a half inches in length which look like little fish, fished between just above the bottom and a foot below the surface. Good flies for surface work on the other coarse fish include Black Gnat, Greenwell's Glory and Coachman. For wet-fly work, for perch especially, a Butcher, Alexandra or Peter Ross will work.

An artificial fly is so light that it is impossible to cast it as you would a bait. Any shot or weights on the line to give weight for casting would make it impossible for the fly to fall lightly on the water and float. The weight problem is solved by using a line sufficiently heavy for the forward thrust of the rod to impart momentum sufficient to carry it forward many yards. We talk of casting a fly, but strictly it is the line we cast, the fine nylon leader and fly being carried forward by the line. This requires a rod and line of a very different kind from that used for even the lightest bait and no compromise is possible. For fly-fishing you must have a special rod and line designed for that purpose alone.

To the roach fisherman, the thick fly-line may appear more suitable for catching shark than half-pound fish. Its bulk is for weight and not for strength. To make it easier for the fine leader and fly to be propelled beyond it, the line is tapered so that its end is little thicker than the nylon to which it is tied. For dry-fly fishing, at least where it is essential the fly should alight on the water like gossamer, the nylon leader is also tapered so that the point is as fine as the match fisherman's hook link.

A fly-rod is flexible so that when it is waved it bends freely. The energy imparted to it as it bends backwards is imparted to the line as it comes forward. Logically, perhaps one should first buy a line then select a rod able to handle it. In practice, the rod is bought first. A good maker will prescribe the exact line it is designed to handle and this is the one you should use. A line that is too light or too heavy will handicap you in casting and never be comfortable. The essential for the reel is that it should be as light as possible. It should be able to hold the fly-line and fifty or so yards of backing and have a check which does not have to be optional, but can usefully adjustable. A guard through which the line passes to the first ring of the rod is advisable.

You are going to carry and use the rod all day, with no resting while you watch a float or ledger. A poor match between rod, reel and line will be tiring as well as making good casting difficult. Therefore buy them together, if possible, from a first-class tackle shop where you can get expert assistance in matching them. Greenheart and hollow fibre-glass are alternatives to split cane for the rod. My own choice would always be split cane which with care will last a lifetime. You will become accustomed to your rod and even acquire an affection for it and long life is therefore important.

The length must depend on the kind of water you are most likely to be fishing. Nine feet would probably be best on the greatest variety of eaters. But if you anticipate mostly fishing lakes and reservoirs a special rod would be a great advantage and this more powerful rod would handle sea-trout and even salmon. On small and much overgrown streams a rod two or three feet shorter is a boon. If you become fascinated with fly-fishing, you will probably end up with three rods of seven, nine and ten feet—but don't forget you will need different lines to match them and possibly different reels!

You will need two-and-a-half to three-yard nylon leaders which may be knotless tapers. The strength of your tackle will depend on the strength of its weakest part, the point to which you tie the fly. Tapered to 4X or two pounds b.s. is quite sufficient for river fish up to two pounds. On waters, generally lakes and reservoirs, where the trout consistently run heavier, you must have a stronger point equivalent to four to six pounds b.s. Reservoir trout do not lie in one place as do trout in running water but swim in search of

14. Spinning for pike on an Austrian lake with snow-covered mountains
for background

15. Spinning on the River Leny, Perthshire

food. When a still-water trout takes a fly he usually is moving fast, and the sudden strain of the heavy fly-line through the water and the pull of the rod, plus the angler's tightening action, will often break six pounds nylon on a fish weighing no more than a pound!

Your essential outfit is completed with a selection of flies in an aluminium box and a landing-net which may be of the clip-on folding type to leave your hands free. There are many other items it is useful to have, such as scissors, etc. But one of the charms of fly-fishing is that you can set out unburdened with anything more than can, if necessary, be slipped into your pockets. I always have a sharp pin for opening the eye of a fly which has been blocked by varnish or dressing.

The care of this tackle is the same as of that used in other kinds of fishing, but one or two points need emphasizing. Whether it is taken down or put up never let your rod lean against a wall or it will acquire a permanent curve ruinous to its action. Have your reel well filled. The reel for reservoir or other still-water trout fly-fishing needs to accommodate the fly-line and at least seventy yards or so of fifteen to twenty pounds backing because fish in such waters tend to fight much harder than those in rivers and make long, fast runs, sometimes going as far as one hundred yards! To discover just how much backing is required to fill it, wind on your fly-line first, attach the backing and wind until the reel is filled. Now take it all off and wind on with the backing first.

The best way to learn to cast is to take at least three or four lessons from an accomplished friend or, better still, a professional. Without someone to guide him in the first steps, it is easy for the beginner to acquire bad habits without realizing it, and once established, they are hard to get rid of. But in many cases there is no practical alternative to teaching yourself, and thousands of fly-fishermen have learned from books.

G 97

Preferably on a still day, put up your rod with line and leader but no fly and give yourself your first lesson on the lawn—not on the drive or you may seriously damage your fly-line. The first steps are best learned away from water where your concentration of the mechanics of casting will be spoiled by the natural interest in the possibility of taking a fish. Casting is easier with a weight-forward line than with a double taper, so get one of those, say AFTM weight standard 7 (the AFTM standard denotes the weight of the first thirty feet of line which is commonly used to work the rod) matched with a rod of about nine feet to cast that standard line. Your tackle dealer will usually advise you on this.

Use a knotless taper leader of about two and a half yards and instead of tying on a fly, use an overhand knot to attach a one-and-a-half-inch wisp of white knitting wool to the leader tip.

Place your feet at an angle of about 45 degrees to the right of the direction you plan to cast and lay out on the grass about thirty feet of line—you can pay off line walking backwards to accomplish this. Hold the rod handle firmly with the thumb on top and facing up the rod. Point the rod down the line and hold the line between reel and butt ring firmly in the forefinger and thumb of the free hand.

Now lift the rod backwards and upwards, increasing the speed and making the whole rod bend with the weight of the line. Use forearm and shoulder power but keep the wrist straight. As the rod approaches the vertical pull hard on the line held in your free hand to speed up its backward flight. Stop the application of power at vertical—the rod will tend to drift back a little under its weight and impetus—and turn your head to see the line flying back over your right shoulder in a loop with its free end on top and unrolling to your rear.

You must pause a fraction to allow the unrolling line to straighten behind before beginning the forward movement. If the line does not travel in a good flat but high trajectory to the rear, you cannot make it do so to the front.

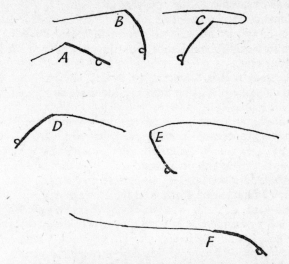

Fig. 16. Six stages in the overhead cast with a fly-rod. A: The line is lifted. B: The road is switched back. C: Pause with the butt upright to let the line extend fully behind as in D when you make the forward cast. E: finally allowing the line to fall on the water as in F

The rod must not drift backwards too far or the impetus given to the line will be killed and the line will drop towards the ground at the rear. As the line straightens to the rear, then, you will feel it pulling on the rod—at that point raise your rod-arm so that the hand is about ten inches above your head and let the hand holding the line move up towards the rod hand about a foot. This allows a little line to shoot back through the rod rings.

From that position push the rod, still pointing a fraction backwards, forwards briskly, at the same time pulling down hard with the left hand to again increase the speed of the line. Keep the wrist locked and the reel at a level above your shoulder, and as your arm reaches the end of its forward movement—the rod should by then only just be inclined to the front—it should still be at shoulder level. Stop the rod by squeezing the rod handle and the line will unroll quickly forward almost on the same plane as it did to your rear.

Basically that is the overhead fly cast and the best plan is to continue practising until the line flows straight and in a tight loop.

Additional distance is achieved not by more power but by having yards of the running part of the line on the ground at your feet and by hauling hard on the line in your free hand, both when the backward cast is begun and towards the peak of power application in the forward cast.

Having hauled on the line in the forward cast, let go of it and yards of the line at your feet will shoot out through the rod rings, increasing your range very considerably. As you gain in ability you can increase slightly the amount of power applied to your casting movement, but do not do so if you cannot maintain good form.

Hauling on the line and shooting spare line is how you can reach distances of thirty yards or more for fishing reservoirs from the bank. In river fishing you may rarely have to cast more than ten yards, and you will only need to give little pulls on the line with your free hand to fish rivers.

When you have some mastery of these movements put down a target, such as a dinner plate. Practise both for direction and length, trying to drop the fly on the plate. Distance judging is partly a gift, but those without it can increase their ability very quickly by practice. Making false casts is very helpful, but, especially when you are dry-fly fishing, you do not want to risk alarming a rising fish by making a false cast right over it and it is better to shoot the last yard or two of line. In practice it is better to be too short at first than too long. The line can be lengthened for

100

the next cast, but a cast that is too long is apt to put down the fish. Direction is generally more easily mastered than the length if there is no wind. A cross wind, especially a gusty one, calls for experience in placing a fly within six inches of the target.

There are alternatives to this standard overhead cast. The side cast is useful because the rod is kept lower, helping concealment and getting the line out more easily in a head wind. The rod is held with the palm upwards and the rod moved in a horizontal instead of a vertical plane. Otherwise the principles of casting are the same. This is useful in getting under overhanging trees.

The switch cast is valuable when obstructions behind you make it impossible to use a standard forward cast. You let the line extend fully downstream and stretch your rod as far as possible after it, dropping the point almost to the water. Raise the rod smoothly and draw off line with your left hand until only the leader remains on the water with the fly running along the surface towards you. Now make the cast towards the point you wish. The free line will swing through the air and its weight will draw off the remainder. End the movement when your rod is parallel with the water. This is easier to make in practice than it sounds in words, but it may well be left until you have had some experience, This will, no doubt, also result in your developing some casts of your own which are not in the textbooks. Especially on some of the overgrown little streams that contain trout of surprising size, the only way to reach the best of them unseen is to forget the orthodox casts. But improvisation requires mastery of the overhead and side casts.

The time has come to apply what you have learned to catching fish. Fly-fishing can be divided according to whether the fly is fished to float or to sink. Normally a dry fly is offered only to a rising fish. You see the dimple or splash of a fish taking a natural fly on the surface and present your artificial so that it is brought by the current over the spot. You can search water on which no fish are rising with a dry fly, but generally when there is no sign of a rise, the fish will be feeding on underwater insects and a wet fly will be more profitable. A dry fly is nearly always fished upstream. Fishing upstream may call for rather more skill in manipulating the fly, but it makes concealment easier. In some of the turbulent waters trout inhabit, keeping a fly dry for more than a second is almost impossible.

Whether you fish a dry fly or a wet fly, the two essentials are that you are unseen and unheard by the fish and that the fly comes to it naturally, which means at exactly the speed and in the way it would come if it were not attached to anything. If the line on or in the water travels faster than the fly, the fly will be pulled unnaturally. This 'drag' probably results in more fish failing to take the fly than all the other possible reasons put together.

Drag will result not only in a fish refusing the fly but also probably in it being scared. When you are casting upstream drag results from line accumulating on the water as it is brought downstream. You may counter it for a limited distance by raising the rod point. But the trick is to draw in the surplus line with your left hand and coil it in your palm at exactly the right speed. This trick is easily acquired with practice. Drag may be caused by the stream moving at different speeds at different points. If the current is faster near you than at the point where the fly will ride, you can avoid drag by throwing a curved line deliberately. The faster current will have to straighten out the bulge before it begins to exert drag on the fly. If you shoot some line just as the fly is about to hit the water, it will fall like a snake and allow the fly to ride naturally for those vital seconds, before the current makes it start 'skating'.

When fishing a wet fly downstream, you can often prevent drag which threatens by 'mending' the line at the right moment. This is done by a flick of the wrist sufficient to throw a bulge developing downstream into a bulge upstream. The movement must not, of course, be so strong that it reaches the fly, which continues in its course unchecked.

Undoubtedly the easiest way to start is to fish a wet fly downstream. For this, two or three flies are often used, the additional ones being tied to the leader nylon at intervals of

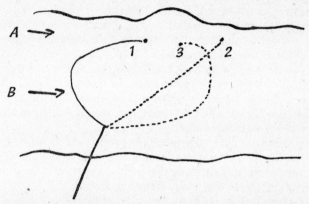

FIG. 17. Avoiding drag on your fly. The current at B in the middle of the stream is faster than at A under the far bank. If you cast a curve upstream as in 1 the fly will not be dragged until it has reached 2. Drag is shown in 3 where the downstream bulge would make the fly skate unnaturally down and across-stream

about eighteen inches. But the possibilities of entanglement are such, especially on a water with weeds or obstructions, that I strongly advise starting with a single fly. Remembering that you are upstream of the fish you are after and therefore paying special attention to concealment, you cast straight across. The current swings the fly round in an arc until it is exactly downstream of you. At this point, it often pays to draw in a little line gently, so that the fly comes upstream. Unnatural? Not in this case because the insect or minnow it is likely to be taken for may dart upstream a few inches. This sometimes results in a fish taking from well under the bank.

Fishing a wet fly downstream you are unlikely to see a rise. If there is a disturbance, it will be too late for your strike. You must strike at the slightest check or tug. Undoubtedly you will have many rises without any indication —this is a disadvantage of fishing downstream and any angler who hooks half the fish that rose to his fly would be fortunate. Better to strike several times to a false alarm caused by fly or leader striking a stone than miss one rise. There are differences about whether it is better to strike 'from the reel' or to hold the line against the rod. At any rate at first I advise striking from the reel. If you connect, there will be no danger of a break from striking too hard. The only result will be a little line drawn from the reel against the check.

If your cast fails to produce any result, move a few steps downstream and repeat. In this way you systematically cover the water. Generally the wet fly is most successful in water that is moving fairly fast or is broken.

Fishing the wet fly upstream is not unlike fishing a worm in clear water in the way I have described, and the trout will be found in the same sort of places. Wading is a great advantage, if not a necessity, and there is no need to have a long line. On the contrary, a line much more than twice the length of your rod is likely to prevent you reaching the runs between rocks, the little eddies in backwaters and other places favoured by the biggest trout. The 'obvious' and most easy places to fish are likely to yield only the smaller ones. For success with the wet fly upstream you need to cultivate an 'eye for water', which is really another way of saying the ability to spot the places where the stream will bring down food to a trout which can rest comfortably while waiting for it. Upstream you cannot cover so much water with each cast and must pick your spots.

When you fish a wet fly downstream a certain number of

trout will virtually hook themselves. Upstream you have to hook your fish. In most cases there will no visible sign of a rise although, if you have good eyesight and can follow your fly down in your mind's eye, you will often see a momentary flash underwater which tells of a fish turning as it takes. Normally the only sign is a momentary halt in the smooth journey of your line downstream. You must strike instantly.

There is a form of fly-fishing in which the leader is greased except for the last few inches near the fly. The effect is that the fly is supported these few inches down, the leader acting as a float. Any rise, even if it is not visible, is indicated by the greased part of the leader being pulled under. A fly can be fished in this way either upstream or downstream, but in the latter case special care must be taken to mend the line as necessary to prevent any possibility of drag. I have found this technique most useful for trout when the water is slightly coloured in streams which are deep and slow.

Greased-line fishing, a term which came from the days when silk fly-lines had to be greased to make them float but which is still used to describe floating-line fishing with small flies fished just under the water, incidentally, has produced something like a revolution in fly-fishing for salmon during the last thirty years. It is a complicated subject with a literature of its own, but briefly it means that in certain conditions when the water is warmer than the air, salmon will rise to a fly fished just under the surface. This can be done with a floating line, and the special flies are very lightly dressed. They will probably strike you as all hook and precious little fly. But the fact is that naturally presented they are effective, in the right conditions. This lightness of the flies and fineness of the tackle necessarily mean that a nine- or ten-foot trout-rod can deal with them and that in these days the trout fly-fisherman who wants to try his hand at salmon does not have to equip himself with a two-handed rod and learn casting all over again. For this method of salmon-fishing, you need icy coolness, for it is essential you do not strike when you see the salmon take, but wait until you feel it.

To return to the wet-fly trout. In still water a wet fly would simply sink slowly and be unattractive. It must therefore be 'worked' and made to move forward by the angler. The movement is imparted to the fly by alternately raising and dropping the rod point, at the same time taking in line with the left hand. It must never be a smooth pull towards you, but a series of sink and draw movements. There is no doubt that the way the fly is worked, which will also influence the depth at which it is fished, is important. The commonest mistakes, I think, are to move it too fast, to make each movement too long and not to fish deep enough. In fishing still waters, incidentally, the temptation is to cast with the wind because it is easier. But often it pays to fish the bank towards which the wind is blowing where air-borne insects and food carried by the surface water drift congregate. Casting into the wind is difficult but made easier by using a short, steeply tapered leader and only one fly. A sinking line may be better than a floater, which will tend to be blown in too quickly and so fish the fly too fast.

The dry fly is designed to float. The fine but stiff feathers used support the fly on the 'skin' of the water and the fly drifts downstream or floats on still water. Casting it requires a little more skill, for unless it falls on the water like thistle-down it will penetrate the skin and be 'drowned', quite apart from the splash of leader and fly alarming the fish. To help the fly float, it can just be touched with an oil specially made for the purpose which ensures it being 'waterproof'. But the greatest care must be taken not to overdo this or the oil will give the fly an altogether unnatural appearance to the fish. Personally I use whenever possible a fly dressed without wings. If this is kept well dried by false casting it will float well without the need of oil and has the further advantage that you do not have to worry about it 'cocking'.

A dry fly is always fished upstream, although if there is a good rise which cannot be reached from below and you can work out some way in which the current can be used to carry your floating fly to the spot from above, there is no reason why you should not try it. The dry-fly fisherman aims to find a rising fish, to stalk into a position where he can reach it and then cast his fly two or three feet above the dimple so that the current brings it down over the fish. With a dry fly you always see the fly taken. It may simply disappear with hardly a ripple—generally the sign of a good fish—or it may be taken with a splash as the fish comes right out of the water. The timing of your strike must depend of the type of rise and size of the fish as well as other factors. Judgement can come only with experience, but generally, the faster the water and smaller the fish, the faster the strike. Bear in mind that your aim is to tighten at the moment the fly is inside the fish's mouth and he is going down and away from you. If you strike as you see the fly going into the fish's mouth, you will simply pull it out. If you delay too long, the fly may be 'tasted' and ejected. Not even the most skilled angler succeeds every time. If the fish is not 'pricked' or alarmed, it may come again. If you find you are missing fish after fish, you can either complain that they are 'coming short', the standard excuse, or you can consider where you may be going wrong in your presentation or striking. One remedy I have found effective on occasions is to replace the dry fly with a nymph.

This is an artificial dressed to resemble a fly at the period just before it changes from the form in which it has grown in the water to a fly proper or dun as the fly-fisherman calls it. Fishing with a nymph is a comparatively new art and science which has received enormous attention, especially on the crystal-clear chalk streams of southern England. Here it has been perfected by some specialists, and although on other types of stream the wet fly may on many occasions be equally effective, nymphs are well worth trying on the fish that can be seen but is not rising freely.

Most of today's trout fly-fishers do their fishing on the many reservoirs now being made all over the country. Most reservoirs are public waters and few clubs have the fishing rights 'tied up'. You simply go along, pay your £1·25, or thereabouts, and fish.

Still-water trout fishing with fly tackle is very different to that employed on running water. It is essential to master long-distance casting techniques, with the double-haul method already explained, for often trout will not approach the bank nearer than twenty-five or thirty yards.

In April and May, and in rough summer weather, or when the hot bright sun glares on a mirror-smooth surface, fish do not generally rise to surface food, only doing so around sunrise and in the cool of the evening. Then the angler must fish his nymphs, standard lake flies, or big lures near the bottom on a sinking line, maybe getting the tackle down to depths of twenty-five feet.

At the same time, when fish are rising, nymphs fished just beneath the surface on a long leader and floating line will produce excellent results, and dry flies are also employed with good results, especially in the gloaming when big sedge flies bustle across the water and a bushy, well-oiled sedge pattern, cast and then retrieved to skate across the water in jerks, will bring big fish up to crash the fly.

As more pollution kills rivers and more water is abstracted from them to quench the growing thirst of industry and an increasing population, more anglers will have to turn from the increasingly expensive river trout fisheries to reservoirs and small private still-water trout fisheries for their sport.

Any attempt even to introduce the subject of fly-fishing in a single chapter must appear inadequate, but I shall have succeeded in my aim if I have pursuaded you that, while it can be made one of the esoteric sciences and a craft at which no man can hope to attain perfection in all branches, it can be enjoyed with some success with limited knowledge and very moderate skill by any 'bottom' fisherman. There are whole libraries of books on specialities and controversies of fly-fishing which have had only passing mention here, but for the most part they will be meaningless until you have had some actual experience of fly-fishing.

8

Sea-fishing

THE coastline of England and Wales has been measured as 2,350 miles and that of Scotland is even longer. Every one of the thousands of square miles of sea along this coast hold fish of many different kinds. Compared with some parts of the world where ocean currents bring big fish, Britain may not be a sea-angler's paradise, but it offers astonishing variety with the advantage that wherever an angler lives there will be good fishing freely available within two or three hours' journey. Until the mid-sixties sea-angling had no great finesse, and until comparatively recently was not considered seriously as a sport except by those who pursued the so-called big-game fish. For many, including enthusiastic freshwater anglers, sea-fishing conjures up a picture of wire- and hook-festooned lines strong enough to hold a boat being lowered from a pier or spinners, held down by weights heavier than any fish likely to hook itself, being towed by a motor-boat. The freshwater fisherman who stalked his trout or roach with fine tackle refused to consider it sport.

But in recent years an increasing number of anglers, many experienced in freshwater techniques, have been attracted to sea-angling with a completely different approach. This has been partly the result of new materials making it possible to solve the problem of sea-fishing with light tackle and also of a more imaginative attitude in adapting freshwater methods. There seems little doubt this movement will grow and 'modern' sea-angling attract an ever increasing number of enthusiasts.

Sea-fishing offers great variety. If some times and places are better than others, there is no close season and the skilled angler will take fish almost anywhere. Piers and beaches may be crowded at holiday times, but for the angler who likes to experiment there will always be places to explore with not another angler in sight. For the family man, sea-angling offers the advantage that his wife's interest is ensured because his catch is always edible and his sport need not mean leaving his children at home because there will always be somewhere nearby where they can enjoy themselves by the sea.

All that I have written about the way fish see and hear applies equally to saltwater fish. The different conditions usually mean that concealment is less of a problem. The angler is usually fishing deeper and further off and, even in sheltered places, the sea is rarely so still that fish are likely to be disturbed by what they see through its surface. On the other hand, when fishing comparatively shallow water, it should never be forgotten that sea-fish, even more than freshwater fish, are preyed on by birds and moving shadows mean danger.

The fisherman on the beach or rock has little to fear that his footsteps will be heard, but clumsy movements in a boat and splashing of oars may result in alarm being spread over a wide area.

The comparative shortsightedness of fish means that the bait or lure must be at the right depth, where they are swimming. That depth may vary from almost on the surface to thirty feet or more down. In spinning or float-fishing, it pays to try different depths until contact is made. If you hook one fish at a certain depth, the probability is that all the fish of its kind are at the depth. Unless you are after fish which always feed on the bottom, it pays even more than in freshwater fishing to search different depths systematically.

The depth of the sea at any point is never constant and the sea-angler is always concerned with the tides. It is a widespread idea, especially amongst 'holiday' sea-anglers, that fish only feed on a rising tide. This is altogether too simple. Fish which live largely on fry follow the tide for the simple reason that fry cannot swim against the tide but drift with it. But this does not necessarily mean straight in and out from the shore. The tide travels along the coast, in and out of estuaries. Tidal currents from different directions may meet. Here fry and other food may be 'held' and such meeting places are likely spots.

Flatfish tend to be carried along with the tide and to do most of their feeding at the turn of the tide, both ebb and flow. The period of slack water seems to be the condition they favour for feeding. Bass come in to feed with the rising tide because it covers rocks or sand which produce the food for which they are hunting. On sandy beaches they sometimes come into a mere two or three feet of water, but immediately the tide starts ebbing, seek deeper water, almost as if afraid of missing the tide and being stranded on a sand-bank.

Most places have two tides a day, fifty minutes later every twenty-four hours. The time of high tide is generally readily available at ports and resorts, and if it is necessary to plan in advance, this can be done with the aid of a reference book such as *Whitaker's Almanac* which gives the times of high tide at the standard ports, with tidal constants to be added for other places. Local knowledge is of immense value, but the angler with an eye for water will note the 'set' of the tide. It rarely goes straight in and out. Headlands, reefs running out and other factors result in it moving across the general line of the coast to some degree. In places it may run parallel to the coast to avoid obstruction. Fish roaming with the tide might work along a ridge of rocks running out into the sea and go out a considerable distance. The side of the ridge on which the tide was bearing might provide good fishing while the other gave nothing.

Especially in and around estuaries, fishing is generally

possible somewhere at all states of the tide. The angler who cannot choose his hours for fishing can fish round the clock if he changes his position and methods. At worst, use can be made of the period of low water for exploring areas which will later be covered by water. The fish will come to the spots where there is natural food.

Compared with any piece of fresh water, the sea is very large and therefore changes in temperature much more slowly than the average river or lake. The day-to-day changes do not normally make much difference, although a spell of settled weather often makes for good fishing. Seasonal changes of temperature are important. The coming of cold weather, as in fresh water, is apt to send fish which like warm water into the deeps which will not be so quickly cooled. Apart from, perhaps, cod, fishing in really rough weather produces fewer fish than the immediate aftermath of an onshore gale. For boat fishing calm conditions are desirable, though when shark fishing a reasonable breeze is required for best results, since the baits are drifted with the boat.

The freshwater angler who takes to the sea will find that all the methods he has used for rivers, canals and lakes, from fly-fishing to ledgering, can be adapted and that sea-angling calls only for the modification of his tackle and techniques. In sheltered waters and estuaries it is possible to use tackle that has been bought for freshwater fishing. But it is probably wise to keep rod and tackle exclusively for sea-fishing because the effect of sea water is apt to be corrosive, and because, especially in a boat, rod and reel are apt to get knocked about a bit. For many types of sea-fishing, the rod you use for spinning with your fixed-spool reel will serve, but it would be foolish to risk straining it when, for instance, you have to cast heavy weights in a strong tide or you expect to pull a large conger from deep water. For fishing from the rocks it is often a great advantage to have a rod of twelve feet or longer. In sea-fishing, much more than in freshwater fishing, the decisive factor in the choice of rod is likely to be the weight of lead it will be required to cast rather than the weight of fish it will be expected to land. If you become keen on varied types of sea-fishing, you will probably acquire at least three rods: a hollow-glass carp rod of about ten feet, which will do for float fishing and spinning, a surfcasting rod of between eleven and twelve feet, with a fast-taper construction to cast weights of between two and six ounces, and a medium boat rod of between six and a half and seven and a half feet, of solid or hollow glass and capable of putting full pressure on line of about thirty pounds breaking strain.

As far as lines are concerned, the choice must be nylon or braided terylene rather than the twisted cotton or flax which was universal until the war. Apart from advantages of longer life in salt water and the elimination of weakening due to abrasion from sand particles working their way into the strands, nylon offers the tremendous advantage of being much thinner for a given strength. The result is much less pull on the weight from the tide and a lighter weight able to hold the bottom. It has enabled the sea-angler to escape from the vicious circle where he had to use a thick line to deal with a heavy weight and the thickness of the line itself increased the amount of weight required. Even more than in fresh water, nylon has brought a revolution and, because of the lighter weights and tackle it is now possible to use, added greatly to the pleasure of sea-fishing. The rule must be to fish as light as is compatible with the minimum weight called for by the depth and strength of the tide. Braided terylene is mainly used for boat fishing, especially in breaking strains of more than thirty-five pounds, when its limpness in comparison to the stiffness of nylon monofilament, and its reduced elasticity, makes it more pleasant and safer to use. When strong tidal currents create problems while fishing from a boat, such as bringing the tackle off the bottom, the use of a wire line will permit you to carry on

114

with success by getting the terminal tackle down with less lead. Your rod must have a roller-tip ring, though.

Let us look briefly at how you can use the common fresh-water techniques in sea-fishing. Float-fishing which will take every kind of freshwater fish has its limitations in the sea. It is not suitable for fishing in deep water from a boat where other techniques for fishing on the bottom or in mid-water are preferable. It may be useful from a boat in an estuary where the tide can be used to carry the float twenty yards or more by long trotting. But it is not the best method for fishing on the bottom, as in fresh water, except perhaps where the bottom is very weedy or obstructed and a ledger or paternoster would be in constant danger of becoming snagged.

The ideal place for float-fishing is on the sheltered side of a ridge of rocks or a breakwater or low jetty. Don't use the 'sea floats' sometimes offered which seem more suitable for marking a lobster pot than indicating the bites of a half-pound mackerel or even a four-pound bass. Apart from the fact that bass are wary fish, an over-heavy float calls for a lot of unnecessary lead. There is no reason why your float should be any larger than you would use in similar water conditions with a bait of the same size in a lake. A small float ensures minimum resistance to a bite. You will generally be fishing at depths that call for a sliding float of the type I have described. A floating line makes for a quick striking and reduced drag on the float in a strong tide. A single weight about two feet above the hook will usually meet the case. The size of hook must be adapted to the bait, but the angler used to freshwater fishing should bear in mind that the unexpected may always happen when fishing in the sea and that if a big fish takes hold, it may have to be kept away from moorings and sharp rock edges.

If you do not have to make long casts, you can use two additional hooks on four-inch links two and four feet above the end hook. This offers the possibility of fishing three different baits at different depths, but I think the advantages are outweighted by the frequency with which the upper hooks become entangled with the line or with seaweed and that it is better to find the right depth by systematic searching. Certainly in the case of mackerel, the depth at which they are swimming sometimes seems very narrow and an alteration of even two feet in the depth can make the difference between a bite at every cast and a blank. If anyone near takes a fish, measure off your depth against that at which he is fishing!

The paternoster, so little used in fresh water, is the favourite method of the 'holiday' sea-angler. I think the ledger is nearly always more effective except when fishing a very rocky or obstructed bottom or in deep water from a boat. In any case avoid the heavy ironmongery of some made-up paternosters. Your paternoster should be wholly of monofilament and a single swivel between the trace and line and another between trace and lead are generally sufficient. When fishing over rocks, attach the lead by a piece of nylon of several pounds less breaking strength than the trace itself. Then if you get hung up on the bottom and have to break, you lose only your lead and not your whole trace. The weak link to the lead does not, of course, affect the strength of the tackle in handling a fish. The weight required will generally be between two and eight ounces, but when boat fishing in deep water and strong tides one pound and upwards may be needed. You detect and act on bites as in fresh water. One of the disadvantages of the wire booms is that their springiness is apt to result in delay in a bite being signalled through the line.

Ledgering is generally the most effective method of bottom-fishing on sand or firm mud in comparatively shallow water. The equipment and method is the same as in fresh water, although the pull of the tides will generally demand a heavier weight and a pierced bullet is apt to roll. A pyramid-shaped lead may be found better on sand and mud. A bomb-shaped lead with brass or stainless steel wires like anchors set near the nose will grip the sea-bed. Some have wires which release on a pull. To make up a running ledger, thread a No. 5 link swivel on the reel line and attach the lead to it. Tie an ordinary swivel to the end of the line and attach your hook trace to the swivel's other eye. The link may be between a foot and six feet long. The link swivel is stopped from running down to the hook by the top eye of the ordinary swivel. Sometimes a bead or short length of plastic tube is threaded on the line before tying on the ordinary swivel.

Drift-lining depends on the movement of the tide and therefore has no freshwater equivalent. Essentially it is midwater fishing without a float and is best used from an anchored boat, pier or rocky projection. The tackle consists simply of a single hook with a moderate weight—not sufficient to carry it straight down to the bottom—one yard or more above it. The bait is dropped in the water so that it is carried away from the boat by the tide. The lead sinks and the bait streams out attractively from it. The depth at which the bait fishes depends on the length of line paid out and this can be varied. When fishing for mackerel the right depth will be between six and eighteen feet according to the weather conditions. This can be a deadly method of taking pollack near the bottom. In this case the length of line must be adjusted to hold the bait two to three feet from the bottom. This will be the depth of the water at the point plus from nine to eighteen feet according to the strength of the tide.

Bass and mackerel can be taken by fly-fishing. Your trout-rod will serve and, when they are taking, mackerel are not particular about the fly, although they seem to prefer one with plenty of white. This is by far the most exciting way of catching mackerel, but unfortunately the occasions when they are feeding near the surface and you have your fly-rod with you are likely to be few. Both these fish and pollack and pouting can be caught by spinning. The rubber sand eel, specially the famous Red Gill, is superb for pollack and must be spun deep. These lures as well as minnows and spoons will take bass which are apt to be wayward in their choice. The mackerel is satisfied with the simplest spinning bait whose attractiveness is greatly increased if a small sliver of skin from the first fish taken is slipped over one of the hooks.

Unless you are after mullet, none of the common baits used in fresh water will be any use to you in the sea. Unless he can obtain his own or visits popular resorts where bait is on sale, baits can be something of a problem to the sea-angler, Most sea-baits do not keep well, and although in these days there are supplies of preserved, salted and even canned baits, on the whole the fresh ones are preferable, although deep-frozen mackerel, herring and squid are much better. If you use them, wash well and then brush with pilchard or herring oil. This oil is attractive to all sea-fish and is valuable for ground-baiting where this is practical. The method is to fill a fine-mesh net or cheese-cloth bag with fish waste, tie it a foot or two above the anchor and lower. A similar bag of ground-bait on the end of a strong line can be used from the shore where conditions permit.

Here is a quick guide to baits and their uses. Strips of fish are the most easily obtainable if not always the most success-ful. Although they can be used with any method, they are generally most effective when moving, as in drift-lining or float-fishing in a sea with small waves. The bait is good for mackerel, passable for pollack, a third or fourth choice for bass. A large piece or whole fish will take cod and is the best bait for conger. The best fish is mackerel because it is oily and tough. Second choice is herring. A fresh fish is important not only for staying on the hook, but also for attractiveness.

Use a very sharp knife or razor blade to cut a strip from the belly where it is light or from the tail where it shades from light to dark. If the strip is not cut cleanly, it is liable to break up on the hook. Cut either a strip three to four inches long, tapering from about three-quarters of an inch to nothing, or a triangular piece with an inch side. Pass the hook through once, leaving about two-thirds to dangle attractively as a 'tail'.

Prawns are a good bait, but in sea-water, in my experience, the boiled red one preferred by salmon is not so good as the uncooked. A live prawn on float tackle is first class for bass. A dead one fished on the bottom will take flounders.

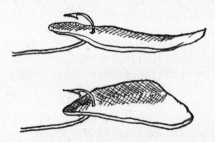

Fig. 18. How to cut and hook a piece of fish as bait

Whether dead or alive, fish a prawn 'backwards', that is with the tail nearest the trace. Pass the hook through the segment in front of the tail from the inside. A dead prawn can be fished on a two-hook tackle. It is apt to break up easily and I have found fine elastic cotton effective for holding it on the hook without apparently reducing its attraction.

Ragworm is one of the best all-round baits, taken by virtually all varieties of fish and often better than lugworm for bass, pollack and mackerel. Thread the worm on the finest hook you can use taking into account the fish you expect to catch. Always leave a piece free to wave in the water.

Lugworm is often the most readily obtained bait. Thread it on a long-shanked hook, bringing the barb clear of the

119

skin which might otherwise interfere with it being driven home. It is the best all-round bait for cod, plaice, dabs and flounders.

Mussels are moderate to good for most flatfish and codling, but not for bass. Their disadvantage is their fragility on the hook which is increased if they are broken in extraction from the shell. Never smash the shell, but open with a knife inserted on the inside and worked up and down. Use on a fine hook passed through the comparatively tough 'tongue', turned over and then passed through again so that it holds the comparatively soft part. A small piece of limpet can be used to hold the mussel in position. But limpet alone is not a good bait and unlikely to attract anything except rock-fish. The best that can be said for limpet is that dipped in pilchard oil it is better than nothing in an emergency.

Cockles are useful for flatfish and whelks for cod. Cut off the tough disc with which a whelk closes its shell before using it. The crabs which can be a nuisance to pier fishermen are useless as bait, but the crab when it is a 'peeler' or 'soft' just before or after moulting is an excellent bait, especially for bass. Peelers must have back and belly shell removed before use; soft crabs are like rubber. Impale on fine-wire hooks—sizes 2/0 to 5/0—and tie two legs to the hook eye with elasticated thread to secure the soft bait for long casting. Peeler and soft crabs are most plentiful in May and June and in September; search under weedy stones in pools left by the ebbing tide; and do not mix the two in your container.

Some sixty different kinds of fish are found somewhere round our shores at different times, but the number the average angler encounters is not more than a score. The largest are the tunny and sharks whose pursuit is a fairly expensive speciality and requires rod and tackle very much more powerful than anything described in this book, although blue sharks are easily taken on the medium boat rod and multiplier reel loaded with thirty- to forty-pound line. The largest sporting fish is the tope, most often caught by ledgering or drifting from a boat with a whole fish as bait, but also to be caught on occasions from the shore with ledger or paternoster. Its rough skin demands a wire trace next to the hook and this also is required for the conger because of its formidable teeth.

The most sporting fish and perhaps the most fascinating is the bass. It is nearly as beautiful as a salmon, a hard fighter, fairly widely distributed and to be taken by all techniques. It is frequently taken from beaches and rocks. Pollack and mackerel are too often caught by trolling with heavy tackle and much lead. If they are taken on light float-tackle from the shore or by drifting from a boat, they give good sport. Plaice and flounders can be taken by ledgering from shore or boat. One of the most interesting ways of taking flounders is by fishing near the bottom with a special type of spoon in which the usual triangle of hooks is replaced by a single one with a long shank which is baited with a ragworm. The fish is attracted by the spoon and takes the bait.

Cod and codling can be taken in season from boat or shore on a paternoster; mussels, ragworm and lugworm being favourite baits, with a whole small herring or sprat for cod. In the areas where it is found, billet gives excellent sport on exactly the same tackle as you would use for trout on fly or worm. Whiting are not very much more exciting to catch than to eat, but if a shoal is located with a boat, sport can become fast and furious on a paternoster and when they come inshore they are a stand-by for the pier angler at dusk.

These are only a few of the commoner fish which, as the seasons change, provide all-the-year-round sport for sea-anglers.

9

Where to Fish

THERE is virtually no free freshwater fishing in Britain. Many miles of fishing are privately owned and not available to other anglers on any conditions. But there are many more miles which although preserved can be fished if you get permission. On many waters day tickets can be obtained at a charge varying from about 25p to one pound or more in the case of some salmon and trout fisheries. There are several thousands of clubs with modest subscriptions and although many are concerned primarily with organizing matches, many rent, or secure access for their members to, good fishing. Joining a local club is a good idea even if you are not a social or competitive angler. You will not only get fishing rights and much good advice, but also help in the fight against pollution which is now so important. In the case of sea-fishing clubs you will find problems of bait and boats are solved and the information that experienced fellow members can give on times, places and methods is often invaluable.

Before the war the discovery of the rich angling possibilities of Britain often required time-consuming correspondence and research. Now there are an increasing number of guides. *Where to Fish* published by *The Field* is a very complete and detailed guide, which includes sea-fishing, although because it is published at two-year intervals and its information soon becomes out of date, it is best to check on the facts prior to making any long journey. The most reliable sources of up to date angling information may be obtained by contacting the weekly angling newspapers and monthly magazines.

Many hotels have fishing reserved for their visitors and others near good waters cater specially for anglers. The British Travel and Holidays Association have a list of some of them. The Scottish Tourist Board (2 Rutland Place, West End, Edinburgh 1) published a first-class guide called *Scotland for Fishing* which deals practically with the wonderful variety of waters available to the angler north of the Tweed.

Cheap and easy travel abroad has opened up great possibilities for the British angler's holiday. Ireland has such a wealth of salmon, sea-trout and brown-trout fishing that until comparatively recently no thought was given to coarse fishing. There are waters rich in pike, perch, bream and rudd which are almost virgin as far as serious angling is concerned. And in the Cork Blackwater and in the Erne system there are superb roach. Ireland's sea-angling, both from the shore and from boats in deep water, is still the best in Europe, although as elsewhere, overfishing by the commercial fleets has depleted stocks. The best information service for all Irish angling is to be gained from the Inland Fisheries Trust Incorporated, Balnagowan, Mobhi Boreen, Glasnevin, Dublin 9.

Denmark is also attracting attention from coarse anglers in Britain since vast catches of roach and bream were made in the 1972–3 seasons, specially on the River Guden.

Iceland's salmon-fishing is too expensive for most people, and the cost of getting there, and of staying there, is also astronomic. However, if some way round these problems can be found the rewards can be rich. There are superb brown trout, and there is free fishing for them. There are also big charr in the rivers and the sea, and in recent years the sea-angling off Iceland has come to the fore, with halibut and vast coalfish being caught.

Also worth a visit, specially in the autumn when a late

123

family holiday might be planned, is Portugal. There the sea-angling can be excellent, specially if you don't mind some hair-raising rock climbing. There are vast bass, various breams and bluefish.

I mention the possibilities of angling holidays abroad particularly because in many cases they solve the keen angler's most difficult problem—how to find a spot that provides sport for himself with interest and entertainment for the rest of the family! The existence of this problem has now been sufficiently realized for at least one travel organization to arrange special tours which combine sight-seeing for the family with angling for the enthusiast.

Index

INDEX